Ongoing Su

"A practical and easy to implement daily guide for you to build your own foundation for self-mastery in just 20 days"

—Jack Canfield, creator, and co-author of *Chicken Soup for the Soul*

"*Ongoing Success and Wellbeing* is a wonderful and practical book that encourages you to reflect on your own life and set a clear path to be the best version of yourself. As a mental health professional, I believe this book offers what I need for my clients to learn about their inner power and wellbeing. I highly recommend it."

—Alinka Avendaño, psychologist, León, Nicaragua

"'. . . if not me, then who?' this one, I am keeping with me forever. Aanchal hasn't just written and this wasn't just a read; this is the action plan we all needed. Her words are the kind you want to print as quotes for keepsakes. The chapter titles and her one-liners that question you, stay with you even after putting the book down. Aanchal's downs make you empathize with her and her successes motivate you to achieve. Here is a boss babe, chipping away at the glass ceiling, but this time, she is taking everyone along. With activities and anecdotes to go with her words—this book leaves one hopeful, and equipped to succeed."

—Aashni Sawjani, board of governor *De Montfort University, Leicester*, podcaster and radio presenter

"As I am reading this I am already thinking of people who I can recommend this book to. If they only read it and applied what they are reading; it can truly change their lives so much. So many people need to read these strategies. The exercises at the end of each chapter do an incredible job of combining everything that you've read and applying it to your personal life. When you finish this book, you're not just going to leave feeling extremely motivated. You're also going to know your purpose, vision, and goals for your life. And you're also going to have a game plan in place on how to successfully fulfill your purpose and accomplish your goals while continuing to prioritize your wellbeing. And isn't this what all of us are craving inside?"

—Huldah Sheena Samuel, human resources data & systems analyst and stay-at-home mom

"This radiant book is one that will not only change lives but save them."

—Aalia Lanius, founder of *UNSUGARCOATED Media*

"Every word I read came alive. I was experiencing the author's journey as if it were now. You will gain your power back and remember who you are. Through her astounding life journey, you will learn to create your life experiences step by step and to your own heart's desires. Use this as a compass to the unknown that lives within you. I didn't want to stop reading because I liked the energy, environment, and feeling it created in me. This book is an investment in yourself. It's an experience that demands to be experienced!"

—Haleh Houshim, personal coach, holistic influencer

"Life brings a wide range of experiences (and struggles!), and Aanchal Vash's latest book brings a wide range of strategies for facing them. Going through the exercises included in each chapter, I've found that being as relentlessly methodical as this book insists can be a powerful motivator. Like any helpful guide or companion, this book is almost an 'accountability partner' itself. With the research and tools gathered here, I believe we can each meet (and be!) mentors ourselves."

—Brad Northcote, writer, journalist, and public relations

"A compassionate and insightful mind guide to navigate through trauma, grief, and being your hero The author lays open her vulnerabilities growing up as a child in a dysfunctional family and having to deal with so much loss at such an early age. What struck me is how, throughout her life, she chose to stay inspired. She chose to see good around her and create good for others. In this book, she shares the power of that mindset and how to adapt it to cultivate purpose, meaning, fulfillment, and success in our lives by guiding us to be self-aware of our needs and wants and then taking ownership of our lives with practical exercises."

—Huda Baig, product manager

"This book is a perfect reminder for the already successful individual who may easily lose him/herself in the busy shuffle of life. While it is also a great introductory book for someone who is looking to dabble in understanding motivation and develop habits necessary to live an ongoing successful life. I especially resonated with the 3–2 to-be to-do list because of my ability to overthink. I wish to personally thank Aanchal for this creation; you light up my life through your words of encouragement and perseverance."

—Abida Rahman, CEO of *RAH Inc.*

First Edition

www.vashmediainc.com

ISBN: 979-8-9864746-0-1

Design by Melissa Williams Design
mwbookdesign.com

ONGOING SUCCESS & WELLBEING

AANCHAL VASH

Top 10 Indian Women Leaders in Canada 2022
By Women Entrepreneur India

ONGOING SUCCESS & WELLBEING

A DAILY GUIDE TO CULTIVATE FULFILLMENT IN THE PURSUIT OF ACHIEVEMENT

AANCHAL VASH

Co-author of the
Success Strategies and 101 Unconventional Strategies
Featured on ABC, NBC, CBS, FOX

This book is dedicated to both my late brothers—
my older brother Prashant, who passed away from malaria in Nigeria. He introduced me to the world of personal development at a young age—
& my twin brother Tushar, who passed away by suicide recently. Witnessing his suffering and internal battles despite a successful career propelled me to become Mental Health First Aid certified, change industries, and begin training people about fulfillment and achievement. This book wouldn't have been a reality if it weren't for the opportunity of being a sister to two incredible brothers.

Contents

Author's Note

In the last 30 years of being a high achiever, chasing the next goal after another, I have learned that you, *yourself*, can be your biggest obstacle to achieving ongoing success and wellbeing.

I was born in India, raised in Nigeria, and shaped in Canada. From the very beginning to where I am now, I have experienced plenty of obstacles, struggles, and heartbreaking moments that would eventually become my teachers. From losing the most influential person in my life, my eldest brother, to having to identify the body of my twin brother when he passed by suicide, I have had to choose how I reacted to these situations to curate the outcome for what life is today. If I hadn't made thoughtful choices, even in the most devastating of times, I am certain you wouldn't be holding this book right now.

How do you get success and keep it going? What does wellbeing look like for you, and how do you maintain it?

The goal of this book is to give you the guidance I discovered for myself thanks to the influence of a caring older brother. Since Prashant was an avid reader, he would consume a wealth of knowledge from the *Chicken Soup for the Soul* books that filled the shelves of our home. He would read them and teach me and my twin brother important mindful practices such as an attitude of gratitude so we could manage the challenges we were facing at home.

He carved a path for me at a young age, a girl from an Indian community with limited beliefs and no encouragement to understand myself or be myself. He opened doors for me and encouraged me to play every sport possible, dance, paint, write, run, dream, and taught me the power of visualization, goal setting, reviewing, self-awareness, and so much more. These principles continue to be the foundation for cultivating fulfillment in the pursuit of achievement.

One thing I know for certain is that life without struggle is like a book without pages. Accepting this is a real difference maker. Know that life comes with challenges—living is navigating, problem solving, and feeling joy. Decide to brush yourself off, clear your mind, breathe in clarity, and exhale uncertainty. Just be present in this moment.

For all of you debating if you should write that book, start that podcast, that business, not-for-profit, or launch that product or service, I hope to be that influential guide for you. People are waiting to hear your message and gain value from your experiences.

Composed of a foreword by the legendary Jack Canfield, co-creator of *Chicken Soup for the Soul book* series, an introduction, and twenty detailed strategies, this book is a guide. A way for you to discover formulas and strategies to achieve fulfillment in pursuing lifelong achievements.

Though you're ready to dive in and discover its contents—this book was written for the reader to take just one day at a time. Lasting transformation is a journey where you start from where you are and envision who you want to be. Then, you take one step at a time to become the best version of yourself through knowledge and mindful thinking.

This book is just like that transformation process. Though the strategies are short and to the point, read only one a day. Dedicate one day to soak in these strategies that will help you understand wellbeing, stay on purpose, and achieve breakthrough results. Take your time with the activities presented in this book to help you discover how to live a fulfilling life.

The topics in this book are not new. I'm not trying to sell you a book with revolutionary new principles—that would be a lie. Instead, this book showcases concepts you've probably heard before but may not have been able to relate to your life. That is why I share so many personal details of my life throughout each strategy. To not only teach you the reality of ongoing success and wellbeing but also *show* you how I've used each one of these principles in my own life. Even the most tragic stories were transformative new beginnings.

No matter your situation, I know this book has something for you. That is because you can achieve anything you set your mind to. And once you have the knowledge, understanding, and guidance on how to use these principles in your life, you're going to achieve more than ever before. You'll finally understand your purpose, what success looks like for *you*, and how happiness is often a guiding compass to fulfillment and achievement.

Create space for yourself and take the time to not only ponder these topics but also write in this book your thoughts and feelings. Each strategy will include space for you to write notes along the margins or in the blank space at the end.

Coupled with activities and exercises, you'll be able to put to the test the concepts in this book right away. That's why it's important to study one strategy a day so you don't get overwhelmed or try to take on too many new principles at one time. Though you have the desire to see a change in your life at this moment, it often takes small steps and trials to see the shift happening.

My hope for you is that by the time you finish reading this book in the next 20 days, you'll then be so self-reliant you'll be able to create any future for yourself that you put your mind to. I know in my heart that the next 20 days are going to be a game-changer for you.

This book is going to help you discover your 'why' and how to align every aspect of life to your 'why'. You will learn to improve your wellbeing in order to sustain ongoing success.

Before you even begin your 20-day journey, stand at the beginning with an intention in mind. What do you want to make happen by the time you finish this book? What do you want to improve? What new deep truths do you want to understand about yourself? With everything you do, have an intention. The same goes for reading this book.

Foreword by Jack Canfield

For those of you who have read Aanchal Vash's previous book, *Success Strategies*, a book in which she shares the secrets of the world's leading entrepreneurs, experts, and professionals, you'll have already caught a glimpse of Aanchal's many accomplishments. You are already aware that in spite of her having experienced major losses in her life, she's proven that it is easy to discover your purpose in life, which for all of us is to serve others in our own unique way.

I first met Aanchal when she was taking my Success Principles Train the Trainer course. She was one of the youngest students in the training, but she was not the least bit intimidated. Her passion to make a difference and the level of her wisdom at such a young age made her stand out. She was eager to learn and understand the principles of attaining success and how to effectively teach those principles to others. It was immediately clear that she was deeply committed to teaching people of all ages, both young and old, to believe in themselves and their power to make their dreams come true. She knew how important it was to help people empower themselves by taking 100% responsibility for their lives.

This book is a manifestation of that commitment. Aanchal is one of those people who is always studying and learning from the best of the best, and now, she has put everything she has learned into a practical and easy to implement daily guide for you to build your own foundation for self-mastery in just 20 days. As you read this book, you will feel inspired by her life story, encouraged by her enthusiasm, and empowered by the strategies and tools she shares so brilliantly.

As you'll see, this book addresses one of life's biggest questions:

"What is my purpose in life?" Well, Aanchal makes it perfectly clear that that is the wrong question to be asking. Instead, she helps you focus on your passions to create your life purpose statement. And when you know your purpose in life and are led by what brings you joy, you'll then be clear about who you want to serve and how you want to serve them. This awareness of your life purpose is an important and often overlooked starting point for achieving genuine success and wellbeing.

The book you are about to read will take you on a well-designed journey from the fundamental principles and practices for creating a life of success and wellbeing to more advanced tactics. If you are finally ready to take control of your life and achieve your dreams and goals, this book has everything you need to get you there.

Jack Canfield
Creator and Co-author of *Chicken Soup for the Soul®* Series and Co-author of *The Success Principles™*

Editor's Notes

For over a decade, I have specialized in helping authors finish their books in the wellness, success, self-help, and motivational genres. I have worked with big names in this genre like Joe Vitale, Sally Beaton. There have been countless book projects I have completed over the years because I love this genre with all my heart and live these principles every day. But of all these books that have come before this one in such a saturated genre, none come close to what Aanchal Vash has achieved with *Ongoing Success and Wellbeing.*

I was blown away when I first started working with Aanchal, not because of the familiar principles clearly detailed in this book, but the way she explains them for the modern world. I was able to see in a new light how to be truly mindful—guidance that Napoleon Hill and Tony Robbins have attempted to teach their readers and viewers for years but can be easily forgotten without clear direction. The activities in this book to start using these strategies for success and wellbeing allow anyone to change their life around in 20 days—not years.

Her personal stories of triumph over tragedy are awe inspiring. Aanchal is relatable because she is a blooming entrepreneur who has mastered these strategies from a very young age—not later in life. She explains beautifully how to discover your purpose right now and how to align your life to that purpose.

I believe what is most important about this book that I've never seen in any other book in this genre is the balance of success and wellbeing. You truly can't have one without the other. In today's age when mental illness is finally being taken seriously, this book dives into cultivating a healthy mindset as she advocates for mental health awareness.

This book truly has it all and touches on every aspect of success and wellbeing. You can't read this book without being inspired to take action. You can't read this book without being changed. You can't read this book once. You can't live guilt free without sharing this book with others. You can't experience real success and wellbeing until you read this book.

You get the point yet? You need to read this book. *Ongoing Success and Wellbeing* is by far the most meaningful book I've ever edited, and you'll thank me later for recommending it so strongly.

Erica Reed
Reed and Write Freelance

Introduction

"Success is not just money in the bank but a contented heart and peace of mind."

—**Sarah Ban Breathnach**, New York Times best-selling author of *Simple Abundance*

"If not me, then who?" A question I've asked myself at the beginning of the pinnacle moments of my life. When I decided to pursue starting a not-for-profit organization. The moment when I was contacted to do a speaking engagement. As the idea of writing a book crossed my mind. Thoughts of self-doubt came to mind as I questioned who I was and why would people care about what I had to say?

Who am I to be hosting workshops to uplift others?

Who am I to be traveling around the world and sharing my journey?

I'm here to say, "If not me, then who?"

The obstacles I've overcome. The inner battles I win daily. The person I choose to be. If not me, then who?

Just like you might have questioned, "Who am I to have this dream? Why will people care?"

You, too, have overcome obstacles and silent battles. You, too, have experienced troubling situations. You, too, have found a way to be here at this moment.

But the real question is, "If not me, then who?" That is my motivation to continue forward despite the brief thoughts of doubt.

'If not me, then who?'

It's time for you to discover your own why. No matter what you are passionate about, remember this question: "If not me, then who?"

I know that if my father hadn't worked hard to move our family from India to Nigeria, my life would have turned out differently. For that, I will always be grateful to my father. I know that enormous move and many that followed were a part of my success.

Growing up with having to tip-toe around my father was another element that shaped who I am today. For the longest time, my father always seemed angry. It was my older brother who taught me a strategy for keeping up and thriving in that environment. Today, my father and I share a very close relationship practicing the strategies in this book.

There are often difficult circumstances that everyone is going to experience. Just like my struggles and tragedies are unique to my success story, I know yours will be, too. Through all of life's difficulties, success is still possible. It all comes down to how we react to each event in life.

I've seen it happen all too many times with my friends, co-workers, and even family members. They are higher performers, working very hard to achieve success. Once they meet their goal, they feel empty until they set their next goal and the next one. But they don't feel fulfilled.

My twin brother Tushar was working as a Financial Advisor for a Canadian multinational investment bank. He was one of the top-performing salesmen who took a genuine interest in his clients' life. He would outdo his targets and the bank would increase his targets to push him to achieve more. He had a very charming, intelligent, bubbly personality and always found a way to cheer people around him.

On July 12, 2016, he passed away by suicide. He was a 24-year-old, young, ambitious man who had a journal with his 10-year vision laid out. He knew exactly where he wanted to be in 2 years, 5 years, 7 years, 10 years, and what courses he would have to invest in to get there. After I found his journal, I spent nights and days questioning, "Why did someone who was all about personal development and professional growth do it? Why didn't he reach out for help?" These questions pushed me to become Mental Health First Aid Certified with the Mental Health Commission of Canada. A few of my questions were answered then.

Understanding my personal story and the lessons I learned through trial and error may spark memories of your own difficult and troubling situations. That's because everyone has them. They may throw you for another loop as you read on, signaling that complete healing hasn't happened. Or you may be experiencing a difficult or troubling situation in your life at this moment, feeling stuck, discouraged, or perhaps not clear on how to start again.

So, how do you move on? How do you avoid depression after years of suppressing emotions?

It is completely *impossible* to achieve real success without simultaneously nurturing your wellbeing. Success and wellbeing are two sides of the same coin. We can all think of someone who has achieved great success in their lives, even those that are worldwide famous and still decided to take their own lives. The world will never forget the day when the news reported the passing of Robin Williams. Someone who brought so much joy and laughter to others struggled with his own wellbeing.

As you start to dream of what true success would look like in your life, you must also be willing to put in just as much effort into your own wellbeing. Success is meaningless without nurturing personal wellbeing. Your emotional and mental health matter just as much as your physical health and your achievements.

"Life has got all those twists and turns. You've got to hold on tight and off you go."

—**Nicole Kidman,** American-Australian actress

Every event in life forces us to make a choice that results in an outcome. The formula that I have memorized to remind me of these valuable life lessons is *Event + Response = Outcome.* I rely on this guidance from my mentor, Jack Canfield, to become more mindful of my outcomes.

The premise of this formula is that there are many events that happen every day that 99% of the time we have no control over. We wake up on a rainy day. Someone cuts us off on the highway. The line at the coffee shop is so long you'll be late for work if you stay. Events are things we cannot control. Regardless of how well we try to organize our days, unknown events are still going to happen *every* day.

When an event happens, you'll have to make a choice. Primarily, the choice is how you're going to respond to that event. Are you going back to bed because it's raining, or are you getting up and ready for the day with the acceptance that your hair is just going to be crazy?

Are you honking back at the person who cut you off on the highway, forcing you to miss your exit, or are you just going with the flow so you don't get upset before you make it to the office?

Are you waiting in line at your favorite coffee shop regardless of the line, or are you getting something quicker at a new place?

No matter what your choice is, it's your *response.* No one else can make the choice for you, and you alone are responsible for your response to the event. For better or for worse, mistake or not, it's your choice.

And it's that choice that leads to the outcome. Even if it's not the desired outcome, it will be a result of your chosen response. Sometimes when faced with the same event each day, in order to change the outcome, change how you respond to the event.

Here lies the key to changing every aspect of your life that has driven you nuts in the past. When you feel that you're in a rut and can't seem to get out. That you're reliving every day like it's groundhog's day. Yes, even when you are experiencing a toxic work environment, the same event, you have the power to change the outcome.

"I've learned it's important not to limit yourself. You can do whatever you really love to do, no matter what it is."

—**Ryan Gosling,** Canadian actor

I am a digital media and branding expert. My career started in Public Affairs at Citibank, Nigeria, where I was inspired to help start-up entrepreneurs and leaders build a strong digital brand they felt proud of. Today I am the founder of Vash Media (digital media and branding), Aanchal Vash Training (speaking and training), & Reach Out Together Foundation (mental health not-for-profit).

When I began public speaking more and more, I received many emails to come and train people on the strategies I've finally put all in one place—in this book. I have a passion for serving others, offering the knowledge and the wisdom I have gained through my life experiences and through the mentors I work with.

Now it's your turn to discover your passion. To understand what success really looks like for you. How to live a life guided only by joy instead of the trials and challenges you've gone through in the past. It's possible, and I know you can do it. Because I've done it and live to tell the tale.

PART ONE

Fundamentals for Ongoing Success and Wellbeing

Strategy 1.
Self Mastery is True Power

"Knowing others is intelligence; knowing yourself is true wisdom. Mastering others is strength; mastering yourself is true power."

—**Laozi,** Ancient Chinese philosopher and writer

Remember a time when you've woken up in the morning and you just don't feel motivated? You're not feeling good, and the will to get your day started is completely gone. All you want to do is stay underneath the blanket or binge-watch Netflix. How many times has this happened and you've stayed in bed or on the couch longer than you know you should?

Unfortunately, not every day is going to be rainbows, sunshine, and magical unicorns. There will be challenging days when staying in bed or not wanting to get started with your day seems like the best possible solution to tackle overwhelming problems. You can feel yourself in a pool of negative feelings with no end in sight.

But you are also self-aware about how you are feeling and regardless of your feelings, you decide to get yourself out of bed and at least brush your teeth. Even though you didn't feel like it, you did it. By the time you brush your teeth, you realize you're thirsty, but you don't want to leave your room in your PJs. So, you get dressed in your fitness wear even though it seems like a hard task to do.

By the time you're dressed and have made it to the kitchen to get something to drink, you also decide to eat something as well.

Once you've eaten even the smallest of meals, maybe a banana, you realize you're feeling a little better.

Slowly, momentum builds. You decide to do a ten-minute workout. After all, exercise is one of your goals and ten minutes won't take much time at all. You put all your effort into those ten minutes; you are feeling much better, and before you know it's been twenty minutes.

A few months ago, you might have read a book called *The First 20 Minutes: Science Reveals How We Can Exercise Better, Train Smarter, Live Longer* by Gretchen Reynolds, a New York Times Bestseller. The seed was planted, and you are self-aware. So, you pushed to get your 20-minute workout in.

All before 9 a.m. you've managed to get out of bed, eat, exercise, and now are probably taking a shower. You're ready for the day and have banished those feelings you first felt when you woke up.

What just happened here? How is anyone able to escape the darkness of the bedroom when they don't feel like getting out of bed, to heading out the door by nine?

WELLBEING GRAPH

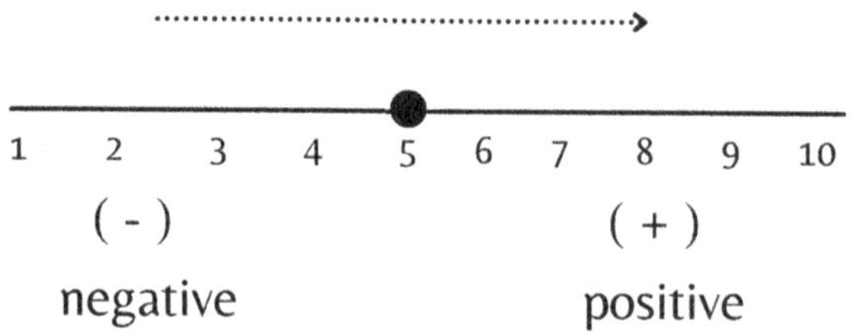

When you start your day out on the far negative side of wellbeing, it's hard to get all the way to the positive side when you just don't feel up to the task. But instead of thinking of one thing you can do to flip your feelings around instantly, you then focus on just one or two things to make the day a bit better. Like at least getting out of bed to brush your teeth. By doing one thing at a time, you get closer to the positive side.

Ever felt like all you wanted to do was stay home and putter around the house instead of going out? Everyone has had this feeling, but we all know that it doesn't get you closer to your goals. Instead, you could spend that time exercising, going for a long walk, or any sort of small activity that brings you joy and helps you move from where you are to where you want to be. It starts with deciding, on a scale of 1–10 on this wellbeing graph, where do you want to be? How do you want to feel? And then ask yourself, how am I currently feeling? What will it take for me to get myself to a 10?

> *"Self-mastery is the challenge of transforming yourself from your own worst enemy into your greatest ally."*
>
> —**Wes Fesler,** American football player, basket player, baseball player, coach of football and basketball

I have experienced many troubling and difficult situations in life, just like you have. The biggest blow for me was when my twin brother, Tushar, passed away to suicide in 2016. While my response was intentional and I continued hosting workshops to educate different communities about mental health and illness; I still had days when getting myself out of bed was a chore, brushing my teeth was difficult, and feeding myself was like an enormous mountain to overcome. I was achieving success with my workshops, traveling to different countries doing speaking engagements, being on the radio, and all that. But it took a lot of discipline and a relentless pursuit of wellbeing to get there—to get anywhere.

I remember receiving a media and communications award in Hollywood, California from The National Association of Experts, Writers and Speakers® shortly after Tushar's passing for one interview that aired on ABC, NBC, FOX, and CBS affiliates. It was an honor to share that moment with my parents. They flew in from Nigeria to be a part of that. The audience was applauding and seeing my parents' reaction brought a huge smile to my face. The event ended, and I got to our hotel room later that night and felt nothing. I opened up my journal and as I was writing, I had a realization that while achieving success is good, a sense of fulfillment is a must. Together, success and wellbeing are soul-filling. From that day forward, I did more activities that I enjoy to add joy to my life.

That is how I created the **3–2 rule** for my daily to-do list. Every day, and sometimes before I go to bed, I create a list of five things. The first three are things that are going to be just for my wellbeing. Exercising. Eating breakfast. Making a glass of celery juice. The next two things are going to bring me closer to my career goal. For example: researching how to gain a new skill set. Drafting the outline for my next book. Working on improving a program to better serve people and create a lasting impact. No matter what two items I have on my list that will help me reach my goal, I ensure I do those two things well.

Overwhelmed! Maybe if I ignore it, it won't exist!

The 3–2 rule differs from the normal to-do list because it limits you to just five items. Oftentimes, a to-do list can become so cluttered and long that it feels overwhelming. We avoid doing any of them by watching Netflix, or cooking a meal, or anything that will keep us from not doing what is on our to-do list. By focusing on just 3 tasks for wellbeing, and 2 for action steps towards your goals, it becomes a manageable to-do list. But it only works if you do each task well and to your best ability.

Not only are these five things beneficial to me, but they bring me closer to my vision; which, at the end of the day, brings me joy. They build my motivation to keep going each day because as soon as I finish those five things, I'm moving on to the next five. I'm moving along the scale towards positive feelings despite how my day has begun or the challenges life or work throws my way. I am intentionally choosing my way forward to ongoing success and wellbeing.

UNDERSTANDING YOURSELF

"Self-mastery is a challenge for every individual. Only we can control our appetites and passions. Self-mastery cannot be bought by money or fame. It is the ultimate test of our character. It requires climbing out of the deep valleys of our lives and scaling our own Mount Everests."

—**James E. Faust,** American lawyer, and politician

Before we dive deeper, let's understand what it means to be well. Wellbeing is a combination of psychological, emotional, physical, and social health factors. It is not just the absence of disease or illness. It is how you feel about yourself and your life.

Throughout this book, we will be exploring the Wheel of Wellbeing—7 factors that influence the state of your wellbeing—including *personal, financial, professional, health, spiritual, giving back, and hobbies*. Even if one facet is suffering and the others are thriving, it tends to influence your overall wellbeing and performance. That is because the factors are interrelated. It may stop you from achieving ongoing success or feel fulfilled because there are parts of your life that are neglected and perhaps holding you back. For example: if you are a start-up entrepreneur, chances are you are wearing multiple hats. You most likely are not just struggling with paying yourself but also lack coworkers to interact with, friendships, a sense of stability, belongingness, or perhaps the lack of physical activity.

Take the time to reflect on where you are right now. You might be reading this book in the comfort of your home, or during your commute to work. Perhaps you're reading while at work, or before you fall asleep at night. Think about how you are feeling. Calm? Relaxed? Motivated? Stressed? Anxious? Overwhelmed? Depressed? What are three small things you could do right now for your own wellbeing that would help you get to where you want to be on the wellbeing scale?

It might feel strange to become so aware of yourself for the first time. That's okay. It's perfectly fine to have growing pains or to feel uncomfortable when trying something new. But I know you struggle some days. I also know you want to see a change in your life, which is why you are reading this book. So, let's take it one step at a time as you discover your potential.

MAKE A JOY LIST

You must ponder what brings *you* joy because what works for me isn't necessarily going to work for you. I feel good when I exercise, learn a dance routine, spend time with my pets, or go for walks. What activities make you feel good? Playing with your guitar. Deep cleaning the house. Reading a book. Yoga. Meditation. Sitting outside in the sun. Rock climbing.

One of the easiest ways to clarify what brings you joy is to list 5 events in your past from childhood to this very moment that made you feel true happiness. What happened? Who was around you? What were you doing?

The next step is to identify if there is a theme common amongst all 5 of those joyful events? For example, the common theme in my 5 most joyful events was out doing my own potential (achieving) and being adventurous (physical activity).

WELLBEING GRAPH

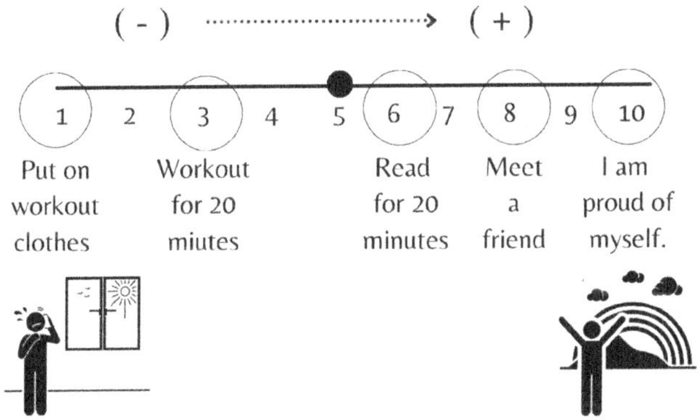

What brings you joy will help drive your motivation to reach the positive side of the wellbeing scale. You don't have to be blissfully happy on days when you don't want to get out of bed. But reaching the middle of the scale and stepping into positivity helps you prepare for what the rest of the day has to hold for you. Do it for you!

Once you decide on what types of small actions bring you joy and will drive you towards the positive side of the scale, then you have to act on those ideas. It's one thing to think about what brings you joy. It's another to get up and do that one thing first that will set you up for ongoing success and wellbeing.

But you only have five seconds. After that, just get up and do it. This brilliant advice came from Mel Robbins and her relatable book *The 5 Second Rule*. After I read this book, I started to say "5, 4, 3, 2, 1. Now it's time to go!" aloud instead of just in my mind.

Waiting any longer and you might miss the motivational drive to move towards joy. Don't waste another second dwelling on the what-ifs of your actions or what is really going to happen when you get off the couch. Instead, start with three things that you enjoy doing before you think of two things that are going to get you to where you want to be. Even if that place is just the grocery store to restock your pantry.

SELF-MASTERY REQUIRES SELF-RESTRAINT

"Those who will not govern themselves are condemned to find masters to govern over them."

—**Steven Pressfield,** American author

If you want to live and create the life of your dreams, master the art of self-restraint. Decide which daily habits will help make the journey to ongoing wellbeing and success more enjoyable—more natural with less force and struggle. Align all your decisions with the Wheel of Wellbeing—*personal, financial, professional, health, spiritual, giving back and hobbies.* Everything else should automatically be a NO. It is not up to your spouse, your parents, your children, or your friends to make those decisions for you. It is up to you to decide what is in alignment with the life you say you want to live.

For example, we all know that one person who can drink 8 cups of coffee a day with the excuse that they are just trying to function. I was certainly that person when I graduated from the University of Toronto and obtained my first full-time job as an Editorial Research Director. I was ready to prove myself by taking on roles outside of my description and getting the highest sales within five months. Since coffee suppresses hunger, I lived off coffee. I woke up feeling extremely exhausted, withdrawn, and irritable until I had my first cup of coffee.

There are plenty of substances that people struggle to resist. Whether it's something as simple as coffee, cannabis, or alcohol. There are plenty of substances in today's day and age, yet very little self-control. It takes a good amount of strength to make the right choice. It wasn't easy to switch coffee with celery juice every morning. Even though I was reading about the benefits of celery juice to boost energy and reduce anti-inflammation, it was hard to overcome the taste. But it took dedication (and affirmations) to make that one switch.

It wasn't until I was taking the Mental Health First Aid certification in 2017 that I really understood how my dependence on coffee was also leading to my anxiety. I learned so much about the impact of substances like substance-induced psychosis that I questioned why people are not taught this earlier on in life. And my vice was just coffee.

My twin brother Tushar had a dependence on other substances that he just could not get to reduce. I saw what it did to him and how his behavior changed over the years. It's too late for Tushar now. But you still have a chance to understand that if you are experiencing substance-use symptoms, there is a chance your brain chemistry can be rewired. Help is available. There are many resources to help you get from where you are to where you want to be and to create ongoing success and wellbeing. It is never too late to decide and build new habits and new results. I believe in you.

Even when you are around your friends and everyone is drinking coffee, for example, you have to be diligent in only choosing actions that add value to your goal. While substances help you manage or distract from the stress and challenges you are feeling, they don't lead to ongoing wellbeing.

"Self-control is strength. Right thought is mastery. Calmness is power."

—**James Allen,** British philosophical writer and pioneer of the self-help movement

You may have realized that the things you've enjoyed in the past may not be good for you and the life you want to live. By practicing self-restraint, you can take care of your physical and spiritual body as you become truer to yourself. That starts by taking actions that bring you joy. You start to treat your body well and then master your mind.

WHY WE WAKE UP THE WAY WE DO

Our brains are receiving over a million messages a day. Thanks to the **Reticular Activating System** (RAS) of our brains, it is able to **filter** out unimportant messages and allows us to focus on the most important ones or we'd probably spend our days twitching from the sheer number of thoughts.

The reason we wake up the way we do has everything to do with what our brain has determined is the most important thought. Whether that is how tired you are, which then leads to the thought that you're going to stay in bed. Or you're thinking about what you want to accomplish that day. Once you tell your brain what you want, it looks for ways to attract, create, and achieve your desired goal.

To really affect the first thoughts you have in the morning, try talking in front of the mirror the night before as you give yourself a motivational talk. You can watch motivational videos right before you go to bed or read an educational or self-help book. This is how you change the most important thoughts first thing in the morning to give you a boost for the day ahead. (In Strategy 5, you'll learn more about RAS and how to strengthen your mindset).

A CHILD OF PERSONAL DEVELOPMENT

My parents moved from the suburbs of India to Nigeria. My brothers and I witnessed the struggles they were overcoming to provide a better life for us. We grew up witnessing some behavioral traits in my father that were very nerve-wracking. Sometimes we didn't know what we may say or do that would trigger his anger.

Thanks to my older brother, Prashant, there was a wealth of encouragement in our home. He would take the time to teach me and my twin brother, Tushar, what he'd learned. He truly wanted to share bits and pieces that would uplift our spirits during the hard experiences.

From having an attitude of gratitude to the power of review (a practice that is explained in Strategy 16), Prashant ensured that we were learning the strategies we would need to overcome the challenges we were facing. It was to motivate and inspire me and my twin to keep trying even though our home environment was very nerve-wracking. Through my brother's kindness, I became a child of personal development and used tools to master myself. I would set goals to help me in school and with sports. I realized the power of affirmations when I wanted to achieve a big goal, and how visualization gave me increased motivation and self-belief that I can make it happen.

Not every one of my goals has turned out as perfect as I could visualize them. However, I have learned that it's the process of using the principles in this book that often teach us how powerful we truly are. Just like I know that you have a deep power inside of you that is just waiting to be discovered and utilized.

When I was 6-years-old, my parents took us to one of our friends to play on a Sunday evening. My brothers and I left the building and were running by the street when I saw a big van driving closer towards my twin brother, Tushar. I ran closer to him and pushed him to the other side of the pedestrian walkway. This is where I had sprained my ankle. We promised each other not to tell our parents anything because we didn't want to upset our father.

A month passed by, and my right ankle kept swelling. After experiencing a lot of pain, I reluctantly shared with my parents what could have caused it. I was in so much fear while sharing because I didn't know how my father would react. At that moment, there was a lot of silence before my father took action. One doctor put a plaster over it for a couple of weeks which worsened the situation and pain. I was given many antibiotics and painkillers. But nothing seemed to help.

One doctor said we would have to amputate my leg. I witnessed my father go above and beyond to take me to different hospitals in Nigeria for multiple consults. We eventually found Dr. Vincent who did the necessary scans and eventually concluded I needed surgery at the earliest to remove the internal bleeding. If it wasn't for my father's due diligence, I would not have played all the sports, won all the awards, been able to participate in interstate long-distance races, and danced.

This is an example of how I continued to stay in a place of gratitude through all the challenging events. The narrative changed internally for me at a very young age. I knew the upbringing my father must have had growing up in a suburban small town in Uttar Pradesh, India was tough. I was so grateful for the life he chose for himself and his family.

As a grown-up now looking back, I have a better understanding of intergenerational trauma and I have even more respect for their journey. (In Strategy 6, you'll learn more about having an attitude of gratitude and how it can improve your chances for ongoing success and wellbeing).

As you learn to master yourself first, you'll find that true power lies in you as you follow the compass of your heart.

"A man who is master of himself can end a sorrow as easily as he can invest a pleasure."

—**Oscar Wilde,** Irish poet and playwright

Activity 1:
Discovering Your Preferences

Look back at the wellbeing graph with a scale of 1–10—how can you intentionally get yourself to a ten on a daily basis? To really know how to manage the scale, you have to become more aware of yourself—your strengths, weaknesses, hobbies, likes, as well as dislikes so that you avoid them in the future.

Your strengths. Example: Resilience, priority management, organizing, networking

Resilience
Self Regulation
Forgiving

Your weaknesses. Example: Inability to say no, delegating tasks, impatient, impulsive

Reactive

Your favorite hobbies. Example: Dancing, rock climbing, singing, drawing, painting

Reading
Writing
Gym
Pickleball

Your dislikes. Example: Disrespect, animal cruelty, clutter, extreme cold, extreme heat

When you have an urge, whether good or bad, take the time to acknowledge it and think, "Is this going to help me reach a ten today?" Let this be your guide to feel the true power of self-mastery.

"I am, indeed, a king, because I know
how to rule myself."

—**Pietro Aretino,** Italian author, playwright, and poet

Strategy 2. Taking Ownership

"If you can take responsibility for your own life, then you will begin to realize that you can change it."

—**H.K. Abell**, Author of *Being Human*

Everyone can agree that we all want to be in control of our lives. Yet, there are days when you'll keep wondering why everything seems to be spiraling out of control. You've come up against unexpected events, felt the crushing weight of constant change, and now are stuck in a place that you are desperately trying to get out of.

How does everyone obtain 100% control of their lives when life is often unexpected? You start by taking full ownership of your life from where you are now. This includes accepting what happened to you whether it was your fault or not and choosing an intentional response rather than reacting to the event. This is perhaps one of the most powerful life strategies that will help you in the most difficult and troubling life events as and when they occur. It will help you navigate the narrative from self-victimizing to self-empowering by taking complete ownership.

"By choosing to take responsibility for your life, you will immediately gain an increased power to achieve your greatest potential."

—**Skip Downing,** Author, consultant faculty development and student success strategies

As Murphy's Law states, "Whatever can happen, will happen." This means that there are many aspects of our day that we can't control. Heading out to go to work only to discover your car has a flat tire, or that you have missed the bus. You had no idea this would happen, but yet it still happened. Events can't be controlled.

Instead, what you do have control over is your response to life's many events. You have to carefully choose a response that will lead to the desired outcome that you want. No, it's not easy. But by intentionally choosing what type of response you have, you are taking 100% control and ownership of your life.

Does it serve you to get red in the face when you discover your tire is flat? Will screaming and yelling make the bus turn around? How about when you burn your breakfast, or you forget that you promised a friend you'd meet them after work?

Whether it is your fault or not, you have to take ownership. Make mindful decisions of how you are going to react and what your response is going to be. That is how you choose your desired outcome. You can either make today a great day, or it's going to feel ruined based on those first few responses of the morning. This is one of your superpowers that you can work on little by little each day!

BECOMING AWARE OF THE MOMENT

After studying this strategy, you'll become more aware of your responses. You'll acknowledge the different events of the day, analyze how you are responding to them, and the outcome that you are currently experiencing. Start to piece together the moments of the day and how you could create your desired outcomes based on how you begin to change your responses.

By doing so, you'll be amazed at how quickly your perspective of life can change. Small events that used to really affect the rest of your day, you are now 100% in control of by choosing your response.

By practicing this awareness, you are setting yourself up for success when a big life event happens that may change your life forever. It is during these moments that your 100% ownership of your life will be tested.

"Accept responsibility for your life. Know that it is you who will get you where you want to go, no one else."

—**Les Brown,** American politician and motivational speaker

The day that a police officer knocked on the door of my apartment in Toronto was a day that my choice response was tested. As soon as I saw who was at the door, I knew what had happened. The officers confirmed my suspicion that my twin brother, Tushar, passed away by suicide. I chose to remain in control even though I had many challenges ahead of me.

With his passing, I had to do things I never thought I would ever have to do. I had no help in Canada as I learned about the estate trustee process to become the executor and act on his behalf to close his accounts. Nobody at the age of 24 thinks about registering a will. The process for any family member to attain that one Certificate of Estate Trustee Without a Will is extremely gruesome.

It took time to find a lawyer who could guide me through this process. Plans had to be made for the cremation of my brother so I could travel back to the Ganges to release his cremains with my parents. None of these events I could have prepared myself for. I could only control my response.

Amongst all the grief I was experiencing, I focused on the outcome that I wanted from this experience. I wanted to be reunited with my parents. But I also wanted to ensure Tushar would have a legacy. Through all the pain and heartbrokenness, I created Reach Out Together Foundation, a not-for-profit helping people improve their mental health. Something I know my twin brother would be proud of today.

TAKE BACK YOUR POWER

"Accepting complete responsibility for your life means that you refuse to make excuses or blame others for anything in your life that you're not happy about."

—**Brian Tracy**, Canadian motivational speaker

During some of the most challenging moments in my life, it would have been easier to blame someone else for my situation or complain to my friends about the despair I was feeling. There are any number of people I could have blamed or become angry with during the times both my brothers were released from this life. I could complain to those closest to me about how rough my life was.

But that is not what I did during past challenges and obstacles. Instead, I took 100% ownership of my life and the actions that I took to become the person I am today.

Sometimes you give away your power by blaming someone else for the tragedies in your life. By blaming others, you give away control of your life. Since the fault now rests with someone else, you, in turn, wait for that person to make your life better again. Yet, the only person who can improve your life is you.

Complaining about your troubles will also not help you overcome them. It is like putting a temporary bandage on the trials you are facing. Venting to a friend sometimes helps in expressing your emotions. But if this is your only solution, you'll never have a different outcome of overcoming your trials.

Your partners, friends, or family members are not trained mental health professionals or counselors. They may not know what to say or how to handle the situation. They may react in a manner that may be further damaging to your wellbeing. If you are not gaining comfort from sharing your emotions with them, I highly recommend pursuing professional help or other self-help support from experts. (Read Bonus strategy to learn how to respond to someone experiencing a difficult or troubling situation)

- Ask yourself what do you need to do to set yourself up for success?
- What is it going to take?
- What are your roadblocks? Is it wellbeing? Is it a toxic working environment?
- What actions can you take to get unstuck and take 100% ownership of your life?

COMPARISON IS A THIEF OF JOY

"The only person you should try to be better than is who you were yesterday."

—**Victoria Vanriele**, athlete

Often when we look at others who are living the life we want to live, we end up comparing ourselves to others. It is a huge downfall because when you are focused on the life of someone else, you end up focusing your energy on jealousy and discomfort instead of raising yourself up. You can either look at the success of others as an inspiration for yourself to take action towards your own goals. Or, you can use that outward reflection to compare to your own downfalls. You are able to see the aspects of your life that perhaps you weren't aware that you wanted to improve.

And let's not forget that person you may be comparing yourself to because they are a great public speaker or have beautiful hair or a strong confident voice. That person may be looking at you and comparing themself to you over your style, your intelligence, or your humor.

While I understand it's difficult to not compare yourself to others, especially in this digital era, you have to intentionally change your thoughts or find a healthier way to communicate.

Let go of comparison and focus on yourself.

Improve your own skills. Remember this formula from the introduction of this book—Event (E) + Response (R) = Outcome (O)? It continues to help me navigate difficult and troubling ongoing life events.

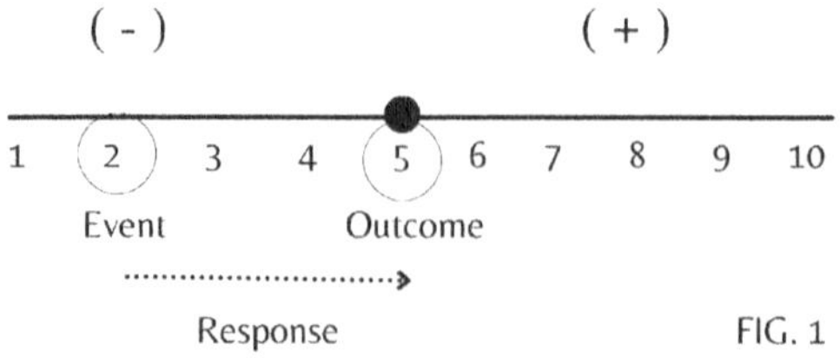

FIG. 1

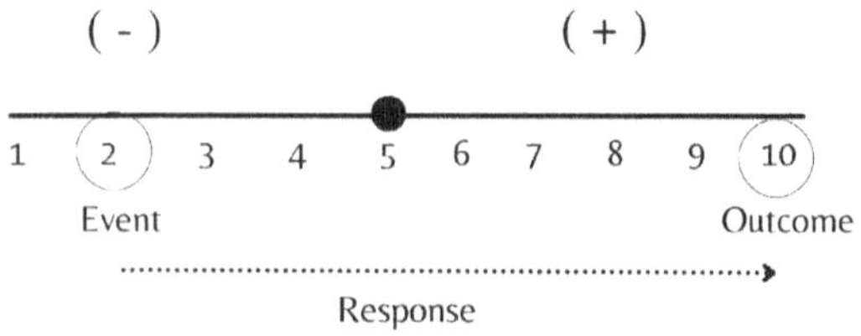

FIG. 2

While looking at the wellbeing graph above—if you experience an event that is a 2 and the result of that life event is giving you a 5 and you are experiencing feelings of unhappiness, that is probably because your response was a 3 (Fig. 1). You have to do something differently if you want to achieve a 10. So, how are you going to make it a 10 if life is still giving you a 2? You will need an 8 response to get there (Fig. 2). The response is the only thing that you have control over. That's how you take ownership of your life and the results you produce.

INTUITION IS FREE KNOWLEDGE

Tuition is the knowledge that we pay for. **Intuition** is the knowledge we receive from within us. It's the gut feeling. When we don't listen to those internal signals and make a mistake, we get into situations that don't make us happy and we can blame external circumstances.

Instead of tuning in, we are guided by external messages. It's a natural process until you start to become more aware of your gut feeling. It's there to serve you. Believe in yourself and the messages you're receiving.

Believe it or not, it's okay to feel jealous. Just like we have positive emotions, we also feel plenty of negative ones. Jealousy is a form of intuition, telling you that there are parts of you that want to achieve those results, or something is missing in your life that you may want. But you haven't voiced it or acknowledged it yet.

Feelings like jealousy, anxiety, discomfort, and sadness are what make us human, even though society teaches us that we shouldn't have any negative feelings. Yet, feelings like jealousy and anger are normal to experience. We simply learn how to navigate through them so they don't disturb or add more roadblocks to success or wellbeing.

I have a friend who is super fit. She eats very well and is athletic in every regard. The way she creates boundaries in her life is something that I am in awe of. I recognized that slight jealousy inside because I realized that I want to be like that and feel fit as well.

My solution was to communicate those feelings to my friend. I expressed freely that I was in awe of her and to keep moving forward. I said, "You are doing everything in your power to set yourself up for success." I'm rooting for my friend instead of holding onto that jealousy and suppressing it. I want to encourage her to just be herself because she's inspiring people around her.

LEARN FROM FAILURE. DON'T BECOME IT.

"I have not failed. I've just found 10,000 ways that won't work."

—**Thomas Alva Edison,** An American inventor and businessman

It's very common and human to fail. No one has made it through life without failing more times than anyone could count. It's a part of life. We all must fail to learn. More often than not, we must try, fail, learn, try again, and grow. Some hold on to failure and wear it as an attire. You repeat it, share it everywhere you go, withdraw from trying again; not willing to let go of the narrative. As a result, the emotions you experience keep you from achieving a different outcome. In fact, a research study in Inc Magazine reveals that the fear of failure topped the list of phobias. In that research study, about 49% of adults disclosed that the fear of failure "was the biggest roadblock to either not achieving their goals at all or discouraging them from revisiting their goals."

Think of the friend who complains to this day about the sports team they could have played on if not for an injury in college? Or the colleague who missed their shot of having a major position in a large corporation? Or the person who missed out on confessing their feelings for the person they love, only to watch them marry another? Or someone's partner leaving them because of their anger issues? Or losing the respect from a family member because of someone's substance use problems? Or someone not making their sales target because they didn't make enough phone calls?

There are moments in our lives where we will feel the weight of failure resting heavily on our shoulders. No one likes to fail, especially when our parents and society look so heavily towards our accomplishments. We might even try to hide our failures, suppressing our feelings.

But failure is only a moment in the grand scheme of life. We move on with the choice of either holding onto that failure and the feelings associated with it, or we use that experience to learn from it. It is often our greatest failures that lead to the biggest achievements.

Can you imagine if J.K. Rowling had quit after her 12th rejection of *Harry Potter and the Philosopher's Stone*? In her commencement speech at Harvard, she said, "I was jobless, a lone parent, and as poor as it is possible to be in modern Britain, without being homeless." She shared how she was experiencing clinical depression and contemplated suicide until she woke up one day wanting to seek professional help. She started using writing as her outlet and today she is one of the richest people in England with a net worth of roughly $1 billion.

"Failure is another steppingstone to greatness."

—**Oprah Winfrey,** American talk show host, television producer, actress, author and philanthropist

Did you know Oprah Winfrey was fired from an early job as a television news anchor?

Albert Einstein had the label "mentally slow" on his permanent school record.

Walt Disney was fired from his job at a newspaper early in his career —they said he lacked imagination.

The greatest basketball player of all time, Michael Jordan, was cut from his high school team.

Imagine if Oprah Winfrey, Albert Einstein, Walt Disney or Michael Jordan had quit learning from their failure. Our world would not be the same without their perseverance. You too can be the next greatest writer, inventor, athlete, politician, or businessman. You simply have to decide to never give up, commit to lifelong learning, and embrace yourself a little more during turbulent times. Remember, the outcomes you are producing are based on your responses. Not the events.

NAVIGATING F.E.A.R

I had the privilege to grow up with two incredible brothers. They both were very inclusive of me joining their playtime in the evenings. Even though there were no girls around, I participated in every and any sport they played. Eventually, I became the fastest runner in my school in Nigeria, played inter-state table tennis, joined the basketball team, played badminton, and all track and field sports that were offered by my school. Whether I knew how to or felt confident, I would participate, nevertheless.

Some sports were intimidating to play in front of so many boys. I still tried my best. I would attempt the high jump even though I was wearing a skort. I was nervous with so many people staring at me every time I attempted a new sport. But I would end up doing it anyway because I knew that I would never learn if I didn't try.

There were plenty of times that I wouldn't make it over the hurdle and trip over while wearing that skort, but I would learn from it, practice, and do it again anyway. I would watch the boys who would win in those sports, and I would apply what I was learning to my own training to eventually win.

What I learned about fear at a very young age is that it's false evidence appearing real. Say that again in your mind. FALSE evidence appearing REAL. How often is it easy to confuse reality with a false version when we are afraid? The reality is there is no true threat of danger or threat of loss of someone dear to us. There is nothing to be fearful of. It is simply an illusion that we create in the mind.

You're afraid of confessing your love because you might be rejected.

You're afraid of applying for that new position because you'll be laughed at by your colleagues for trying.

You're afraid of traveling to a new country because of all the unknowns.

But fear is just a false version of reality. You truly don't know what the event is going to be until you see for yourself by taking action. You can only choose the response when the time comes to have the desired outcome you really want.

And if you don't try, you could live a life full of regret. Therefore, don't let fear rule your mind. Instead, take 100% ownership of the outcomes you produce and practice being ferociously brave. In reality, what do you have to lose? Nothing but a moment of time that will still lead to the next.

"We generate fears while we sit. We overcome them by action."

—**Dr. Henry Link,** Famous psychologist and best-selling author in 1936, *The Return of Religion*

An inspirational, true story that serves as an instant motivator for anyone out there that has gone through trials and tribulations in life is *F.E.A.R* by Brittney Carr. This book was designed to help the millions of people worldwide that are currently going through something very difficult in life such as physical health issues, mental illness, financial problems, anxiety, addiction, heartbreak, failed relationships, parenting obstacles, death of a loved one, self-esteem trouble, spiritual warfare, mental/emotional trauma and much more. Each of these things has one thing in common; they thrive and survive on our FEAR.

SELF-COMPETITION

My first job after university was a sales role for a digital publication. It was a very intimidating role since I was the only woman on the team. I was surrounded by men with strong voices. It was a harsh environment where I had to learn to speak up. That wasn't something I was encouraged to do growing up because women were supposed to have soft, cheerful voices.

During that first five months, the stories I brought on didn't make any ad sales. I struggled with cold-calling CEOs. It was clear that there was no respect for women. I was surrounded by intimidating men who were managing millions of dollars in sales every month.

I had a choice to make. I could either compete against the salesmen or I could compete against myself and focus on the results I was producing. Despite what I was experiencing in this working environment, I took 100% ownership and decided to create a new outcome. I started practicing my pitch in order to make it my own. Every chance I had, I was reciting the pitch till it was muscle memory—on my commute to work, the shower, walking up the stairs or lobby, or waiting for my food to arrive at a restaurant.

Within five months I became the top salesperson. No one could come close to my numbers. Instead of being afraid of trying to compete with others, I simply decided to compete with myself. I knew in my heart I could do better, so that is what I did.

Do you ever feel as though you are competing against others? Perhaps it's the people you work with, your siblings, or even your spouse? Are you trying to get the best job that pays the most in order to outshine others around you?

Bottom line: you're probably exhausted and unhappy. Instead, switch the script. Start competing only with yourself to discover the type of growth that brings happiness. You know you can do better. You have that feeling in your gut that your life was meant to be grander than what you've experienced thus far. As you move forward, know that the only person in the entire world you're competing against is yourself. It's you or nothing.

I am in competition with myself because I am 100% taking ownership of my life and where I want to be. There will always be people better than me, and I am cheering them on. I am just competing with myself, my goals, my skill set, and my dreams. I explore my own potential, which will benefit me and then my entire community. Let the below exercise inspire you to take small steps towards being 100% accountable for your own life, results, and outcomes.

"To be a champion, compete; to be a great champion, compete with the best; but to be the greatest champion, compete with yourself."

—**Matshona Dhliwayo,** Canadian philosopher, entrepreneur, and author

Activity 2:
Wheel of Wellbeing

Look at the Wheel of Wellbeing below and write down 3 things that you will do as taking full ownership under each of these areas of wellbeing.

Sometimes it feels too overwhelming to take on full ownership, then just start with 1% more ownership. 1% more wellbeing like going on a walk or taking the time to see a dentist, therapist, or just playing with your cat. There is so much potential and room for growth that starts with doing just 1% more.

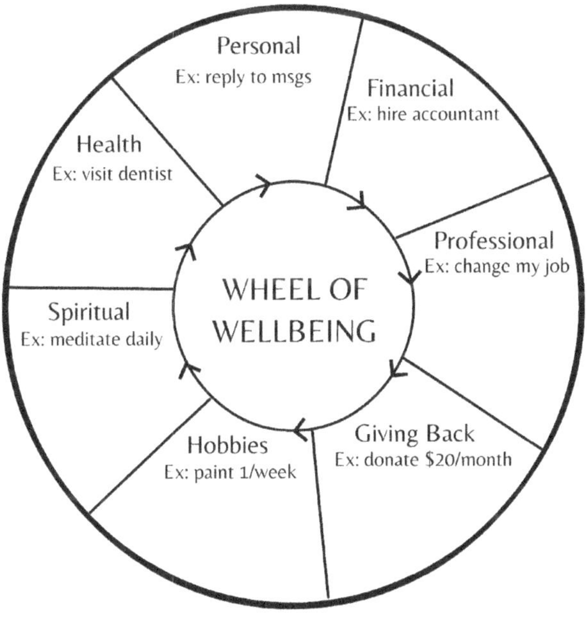

"The price of greatness is responsibility."

—**Winston Churchill**, Former Prime Minister of the United Kingdom

Strategy 3. Define Your Purpose

"The purpose of life is to contribute in some way to making things better."

—**Robert F. Kennedy**, Former United States Attorney General

By reading the title of this strategy, you can already imagine the activity that is going to be found at the end of this chapter. Yet, you're probably already wondering how to define your purpose when people spend their entire lives trying to discover this. You don't have to spend your entire life discovering your purpose.

You can decide today, and if you already have it defined and still finding yourself unhappy, perhaps it's time to define a new life purpose. I once attended a Tony Robbins' training and will never forget these words.

"I will tell you right now, there's one word that will give you happiness, one. You'll remember it as long as you live: progress. Progress equals happiness. Achieving goals does not equal happiness. So, if you're asking yourself, "What is my purpose?" What you're really asking for is progress – a true sense of fulfillment. And fulfillment isn't a luxury or leisure activity – it's a necessity."

~ Tony Robbins

Think about it. How many people do you know hate the job they are working in, but stick with it anyway? Or you have experienced putting years into a job that feels unfulfilling? Perhaps you quit a job and started a business that just isn't infusing joy anymore. You might be retired and realized that life isn't what you were told it would be. We can all agree that not everyone is following their purpose, or even aware of what their purpose might be.

It's time to stop wasting energy on questions like "What is my purpose?" and "Why was I born?" I can tell you the answer to those questions right now.

Your purpose and my purpose are to be of service to others. It's that simple. The reason we were all born is to serve others, to propel humanity forward, and to add value to the lives of those around us. This, and only this, will determine the quality of life that you experience as well as the type of success you will have.

Now you have to decide *how* you want to serve. The answer to that question stems from what your true passion is. The new question you should be asking yourself now is, "*What* do I want to serve, and *how* do I want to do it?"

It doesn't matter if you are a construction worker, painter, musician, baker, farmer, IT consultant, travel agent, realtor, or taxi driver. You are adding value to the lives around you. You are making someone's life better. You are filling a want and need in the world.

DISCOVERING YOUR PURPOSE

"He who has a why to live for can bear almost any how."

—**Friedrich Nietzsche**, German philosopher

What do you want to serve? Whom do you want to serve? How do you want to serve? What activities infuse joy and meaning to your life? What would you rather be doing with your time that would be helpful and make a difference? What qualities do you naturally have that can be helpful to others and create impact? (Use the exercise at the end of this chapter to help you create your own Life Purpose Statement.)

For now, these are your guiding principles for your path to discovering your purpose. No matter what career you are in, you can apply these questions to your current situation. You don't need a clean slate to define these questions. Everyone can create change by taking small steps today.

What do you want to serve? This could be a product or a service. It could be your music or paintings. Your labor, time, and energy. Your own product, or the product you sell for the company you work for. Everyone serves something each day from as simple as a smile to the vibe you give off. No matter what you currently serve, what would you like to serve?

Who are you currently serving? Get specific. This can be customers, team members, family members, and friends. The list of people you interact with each day is those who you are currently serving. It can be a stranger you pass by on the street that you give a nod to in passing. Or it's the tip you leave the barista that makes your coffee in the afternoon. Every day we are serving all sorts of people who rely on us. But if you could choose, who would you like to serve?

How do you want to serve? Time is one of the #1 way in which we are already currently serving others. We share our time at work. Time with family. Time on personal hobbies. You can create an impact by sharing your energy, effort, uplifting humanity, or saving the planet. But if you could choose, how would you like to serve others?

Think about the activities that infuse joy and meaning into your life. Is it hosting orphanage charity visits? Perhaps playing sports or training others in how to improve their performance, diet, or overall fitness level? Or is it protecting people from cyber-attacks and keeping their privacy safe from hackers/spies?

Or is it to spend time with horses, or run social campaigns to protect the dolphins?

What would you rather be doing with your time that would be helpful and make a difference? Would you rather train people on self-help strategies or bring joy and laughter to people's lives or teach people how to become better at selling? You may want to help people build their digital presence and help them with their digital branding. Perhaps teach people how to speak in public and give speeches or share your knowledge about book writing and publishing.

Whatever it may be, it's important to reflect on how you want to make a difference. Since I was a little girl, I knew I wanted to make a difference in people's lives, and I knew my life purpose was to be of service. My parents kept telling me that I should focus on studying, and then I should focus on getting a good job to gain as much experience as I can. While that was all good advice, I had to take the time to reflect on WHAT exactly I wanted to do to make a difference. Ultimately, I am 100% responsible for creating a life I enjoy living. It's not because of the advice given to me by my parents or my teachers or my siblings or partner.

"The great thing in this world is not so much where you stand, as is what direction you are moving."

—**Oliver Wendell Holmes,** Former Associate Justice of the Supreme Court of the United States

What qualities do you naturally have that can be helpful to others and create impact? Everyone has unique qualities and traits that they can use to serve others. Even being a good listener is a way to serve others. Or caring, your kindness, ability to be positive, calm, or naturally good at uplifting people are ways to be of service. But if you could choose, what would be your unique qualities?

As you've read through those questions, you're starting to

think of how you're currently serving versus the way in which you'd like to serve others in the future.

Here are a few examples of a Life Purpose Statement to get you digging deeper:

- To bring joy and laughter through humor.
- To stand up for issues that I believe in and to contribute positively to my community. I want to leave the world knowing that I made it a better place.
- To bring more convenient and functional technology to the world that will improve the quality of life
- To build a loving home with my family and to care for my children.
- To harness my creativity and imagination to unearth truths about myself, my community, and society at large.
- To empower and inspire others to live a life where they are mentally and physically healthy and have peace and contentment.
- To help organizations achieve their highest goals in the most effective way possible.
- To nurture my creative talents and help others find theirs.

If you're still not quite sure what that looks like yet, that's okay. There is no need to get upset, discouraged, or feel alienated. It just means you have to continue to uncover your repressed choices that are buried so deep down to bring them to the surface. While mindful meditation is a great way to reflect on each of the questions listed in the exercise, the below strategies also help with understanding your purpose. You have a beautiful purpose that you are now discovering. It will pave the way to embrace the foundation for your success and wellbeing.

As stated in Forbes, *Three Simple Steps to Identify Your Life Purpose And Leverage It In Your Career*, "Make it very simple and straightforward, and don't overcomplicate it. And realize that it can have a self-oriented focus, meaning that it can be about where you personally find joy . . . The key to uncovering your life purpose is to start behaving as if you're worthy enough to have one."

BE OPEN TO CHANGE

I often say that happiness is my guiding compass. If it doesn't bring me joy, then I don't include that in my life. Even though cleaning the house can feel like a chore, the joy of having a clean space is well worth the effort.

Many people believe that money will lead to happiness. Therefore, they work really hard in good-paying jobs only to discover that money is not the answer. It definitely helps us pursue hobbies or helps us create a bigger impact that brings us joy. But money in itself isn't happiness. I've worked for digital publications and ad tech companies where my team members were making a hefty salary each year. But despite the comfortable amount they were making, they still expressed how unhappy they were to me. I found that they were living unfulfilled lives despite all the money in the world.

There came a time in my own life when that thirst for money did not fulfill my purpose anymore. My parents worked very hard to offer their children a life they did not grow up having. And witnessing the gender disparities and inequalities during my upbringing encouraged me to always be financially independent. So, when I moved to Canada at 17-years-old with Tushar for our undergraduate studies, I got a job right away and started saving to invest.

My life purpose until 2016 was to be financially independent and never rely on a partner to provide for me. But six months after my twin brother passed away to suicide, what once brought me joy just did not anymore. I knew I had to change something. So, I took 100% ownership of my life and realized it was time to start over.

It was time to change my life's narrative and create a new purpose. I chose to get certified as a Mental Health First Aider with the Mental Health Commission of Canada and immediately started hosting educational trainings across the world to educate and train people on how to maintain good mental health. There was no laid path for me, but with this intention to serve others through sharing my knowledge, I was able to rediscover my new purpose. I wasn't making the kind of money I used to, but I was happy putting in the hours to make a difference in the lives of different communities.

I changed my purpose from being financially driven to impact-driven. I realigned my new purpose to be of service and uplift people who were experiencing difficult and troubling situations in their jobs, businesses, families, relationships, and who had also experienced sudden and unexpected loss. I was following my passion and the joy that this new experience brought me. That is how I know you can do the same.

FOLLOW YOUR PASSION

As far back as the fourth century BC, the Greek philosopher Aristotle was inquiring about the idea that everything in life has a purpose, and that purpose is to attain some good. He pondered over what true happiness is and argued that happiness is our ultimate purpose.

To summarize from *Pursuit of Happiness* (2018), according to Aristotle, the purpose and ultimate goal in life is to achieve eudaimonia ('happiness'). He believed that eudaimonia was not simply virtue or pleasure, but rather it was the exercise of virtue.

Oftentimes we might pursue a passion only to discover it's not our purpose. Your list of things that bring you joy will be a good starting point to understand what you are passionate about.

And when you're not sure, you can try a few ideas to see what your true passion is. One of the best ways is to volunteer in those roles to gauge your continued interest. Use joy as a compass to understand if you are on track or off track. In today's fast-paced, technology-driven world where we are being pulled in many directions all at once, finding the purpose of life seems more important than ever.

> *"It's the choice. You have to wake up every day and say, 'There's no reason today can't be the best day of my life.'"*
>
> —**Blake Lively,** American actress

Activity 3:
Write Your Life Purpose Statement

Having a purpose statement is an important guiding factor in your life. Once you have developed your purpose statement, you are able to decide if a task or an event aligns with this purpose. If not, you know how to respond. You tell someone no when they ask you to take on a new project. Realizing that mountain of work doesn't align with your purpose helps you say no instead of just agreeing.

As you develop your purpose statement, you'll focus on your values, beliefs, as well as your passions. Think about what is really important to you, and not someone else. Self-discovery is a process that leads you to living a fulfilling life.

As you develop your first purpose statement, consider your skills and talents, along with what you like and dislike. This process is going to bring you closer to a level of self-appreciation you might not have practiced before.

What I love about having a clear purpose statement is that it will keep you on track. You'll avoid wasting time making decisions or carrying out behaviors that do not provide you with what you really want out of life and how you want to contribute to the world.

Your purpose statement can help you take the initiative to gain the skill set you've always wanted, or to pursue a career far different from what you've currently experienced.

This purpose statement will be a reflection of who you are and will help you stick with it, no matter what someone else might say to convince you otherwise.

Consider these questions below to help guide you towards that final statement.

1. What do you want to serve? Example: Service/ product/ volunteer/ hope

____

2. How do you want to create impact? Example: Uplift humanity/ save the planet

____

3. Whom do you want to serve? Be specific. Example: Young professionals/ horses

____

4. What activities infuse joy and meaning to your life? Example: Playing sports/ teaching

____

5. What would you rather be doing with your time that would make a difference? Example: Educating people about self-help strategies/ bring joy and laughter

____

6. What qualities do you naturally have that can be helpful to others and create impact? Example: Caring/ Positivity/ Calm/ Public Speaking/ Uplifting people

____

Now it's time to write your purpose statement by bringing together the answers to the questions above.

Example: *My life purpose is to empower young professionals experiencing difficult and troubling situations with self-help strategies to achieve ongoing success and wellbeing.*

Below, write your purpose statement.

____

Know your purpose statement like the back of your hand. It will become the guiding force in your life that will lead you to discover your place in the world

"It is never too late to be what you might have been."

—**George Eliot,** English novelist, poet, journalist, one of the leading writers in the Victorian Era

Strategy 4. Nurture Relationships

"Personal relationships are the fertile soil from which all advancement, all success, all achievement in real life grows."

—**Ben Stein**, American writer, lawyer, actor, comedian, and commentator

I left my job 5 years ago. In the beginning, it was thrilling. But with the workload increasing, I soon realized that success is a team sport. By that, I don't only mean building a powerful team of key staff, but also building your dream team of social connections, health connections, spiritual connections, financial, a team of change makers, and a team of people to have fun with. This dream team will help you achieve ongoing success and wellbeing in the face of troubling and difficult situations.

The reality is that we are living in a time of true disconnection. With the rise in popularity of Wi-Fi and social media, most people's attention has shifted to attract more online friends, followers, and subscribers. While technology may be connecting us more than ever virtually, it is also disconnecting us from nature, from real people, and from ourselves. Consider this: how many people from your online friends list would be at your side in a heartbeat if you needed them? How many people would show up during a crisis?

Relationships are crucial for achieving ongoing success and wellbeing. When we nurture relationships, they in turn should nurture us. We are not meant to play the life game alone. Let's dive deeper into what your dream team should consist of.

"I've learned that people will forget what you said, people will forget what you did, but people will never forget how you made them feel."

—**Maya Angelou,** American poet, memoirist, and Civil Rights activist

SOCIAL CONNECTIONS

Complete wellbeing includes the state of your social life. According to Stanford Medicine's landmark study, they showed that the lack of social connection is a greater detriment to health than obesity, smoking, and high blood pressure.

On the other hand, strong social connections lead to a 50% increased chance of longevity, increased strength in the immune system, and the ability to recover from disease faster.

Check up on your social health by reflecting on the condition of your current relationships. Do you have strong relationships that are healthy and joyful or relationships that can be troublesome and stressful? An article by the Mental Health Association of Canada explains what happens when we are isolated or feel lonely. We experience higher levels of anxiety, depression, lower self-esteem and empathy, and a lower immune system.

Good quality connections are vital to your health. Being able to freely communicate with people, being yourself, sharing moments of laughter, eating together, and relying on friends during your time of need, and in turn, being there for your friends is a balanced relationship. It's a give-and-take system that should never be one-sided.

10 ways to improve your social connections are . . .

- Join a local community group

- Volunteer for a cause
- Try out a group activity
- Start a club or join a club
- Invite a coworker for drinks or lunch
- Get to know your neighbors
- Express gratitude to strangers
- Teach something you know to underprivileged communities
- Host dinner parties
- Call an old friend once a week

Just because you may be an introvert doesn't mean you are exempt from social interaction. Recent research by psychology professor Barbara Fredrickson shows that even casual positive interactions with acquaintances can cause a major lift in spirits. If you are lonely, remember there are over 7 billion people in this world. We all need real connections.

PROFESSIONAL CONNECTIONS

In order to grow professionally and take your career to the next level, invest in growing your professional relationships. This is as equally important as having deep connections with friends and family. Society is stuck with the way things used to be in the workplace with formal work relationships. Now, the dynamic of business relationships has changed to being more sincere while increasing productivity.

My relationships in the workplace are not all formal. We've learned to be serious during hard working hours but can also communicate on a deeper level to improve trust, performance, and to create a fun working environment. According to a Great Place to Work, an organization that rates the top twenty-five greatest companies to work for in the world, their Trust Model consists of the five dimensions of credibility, respect, fairness, pride, and camaraderie. By incorporating these into your work environment, you'll be able to connect deeper with your coworkers.

6 ways to improve your professional connections are . . .

- Organize a team networking lunch once a month.
- Take interest in your team's lives, results, and/or any roadblocks they are facing.
- Make a list of professionals outside your work you want to network with.
- Share articles or resources that may be of interest to people in your professional network.
- Attend professional conferences or trade shows.
- Use LinkedIn to connect with professionals internationally.

When I was working in stressful environments, it was the quality of relationships that helped me work in a tough toxic space. I am still friends with many that I worked with because of the deep relationships I created by taking the initial step. You never know when you'll work with these past relationships. Many of these individuals from the digital publication to ad tech network now work at my company, Vash Media, or volunteer at my mental health not-for-profit, Reach Out Together Foundation.

Take the initial step to establishing strong professional relationships. Choose the desired outcome, especially if you are not happy with where you are professionally. Initiate conversations that go beyond normal work. Show your coworkers you truly care about them and are grateful for them.

HEALTHCARE CONNECTIONS

Dr. Michael Balint stated, "The doctor herself/himself is the most frequently prescribed medication." In other words, the physical interaction between the patient and the doctor is as important as the medication that is being prescribed. If the medical doctor is not conscious of the way they engage with their patient, they will miss the opportunity to provide true healing.

Creating a network of health professionals you can rely on

is important to your overall health. Gather a team that will set you up for success with your health. You may have a friend who is a nutritionist, physical therapist, chiropractor, psychologist, or family doctor. There are many professionals in your community who are going to support you and your wellbeing.

By creating deep connections with healthcare professionals, you are moving beyond the normal twenty-minute visit where you are just describing your symptoms. Take the first step to really get to know these healthcare professionals. Be willing to offer just as much as you are expecting from them. This will create that deep connection that goes beyond referring to each other by last names. There are many benefits of knowing everyone in the health network on a first-name basis.

9 tips for improving your communication with your healthcare provider . . .

- Be prepared for the appointment by having a list of 2–3 goals to talk about.
- Bring a friend with you that can help ask questions you might be reluctant to ask.
- Prioritize your problems.
- Share your chief concerns, not complaints.
- Ask for your provider's email as a means to establish easier communication.
- Give your provider a chance to problem-solve when facing a tricky diagnosis.
- Be completely honest with your provider to establish trust.
- Seek to understand from your provider's perspective.
- Pay attention to your body language during appointments.

Everyone should take the time to invest in a therapist. We cannot succeed without help from others and having an unbiased professional to talk to will aid you in strengthening your mental health. Five years ago, when I quit my job to start my first business, I was so overwhelmed with processing the death of my twin brother, working with the Superior Court of Justice to become his executor, wrapping up his legal paperwork, running my organization, motivating the team, hosting training seminars, and so much more. It felt right to invest in a therapist for the very first time.

I changed four therapists, but I didn't quit on my wellbeing. Something told me, "This isn't the one." Eventually, I started working with someone whose energy level was as high as mine. I absolutely loved visiting her. We got to a point, where you couldn't tell if I am her therapist or if she is mine.

When you network with a group of friends who are all experts, you are able to obtain a great wealth of knowledge and advice from those that you can trust to provide a good source of information. We are all experts in something, and therefore can offer others value as well. When we all work together, we make up a sum that is greater than just one flaw.

SPIRITUAL CONNECTIONS

There are people in our community who have a wide range of spiritual backgrounds. Even if that spirituality differs from your own beliefs, it's important to keep even these people in your close network because they have different skill sets.

Suzanna Degges-White, a licensed counselor and professor at Northern Illinois University states, "When it comes down to it, the people we like to be around are those who make us feel good about who we are, what we believe, and what we enjoy doing. Although not every friend will meet all of those preferences all the time, the ones who support the aspects of our identities that matter the most are the ones we are most likely to count among our collection of good friends."

The top five reasons to have spiritual connections are . . .

- To learn new healing practices

- Gain a unique perspective on your difficult circumstances
- Receive encouragement and guidance on how to move forward
- Experience new uplifting practices
- Discover a deeper sense of peace and harmony

When I was going through several difficult trials in my life when I knew there was no one that could help me, I relied on spirituality and the growth that it offered me. Those in my network that are spiritual guided me through a process of healing when I needed it most.

One of my friends who is spiritually strong offered to smudge the condo that my brother passed away in. It was so hard to keep good tenants after I rented out the space, but once my friend burned sage and conducted a healing ceremony in the space, I felt an overwhelming sense of peace I never thought I'd experience again there. To this day, I have wonderful tenants. I have peaceful feelings towards that condo thanks to the spiritual practices of a good friend.

FINANCIAL CONNECTIONS

There are important financial advisors who are already in place for you. You just need to be on the lookout for them. They offer services to set you up for financial freedom. You'd be surprised how many free services your bank already offers. Finding the right people to work with for your financial health will take you to the next level. But you have to start now instead of putting this relationship on the back burner.

Tara Well, Ph.D., an associate professor of psychology at Barnard College at Columbia University says, "while money can't buy happiness—it can buy more control."

When I was in university working at a restaurant and doing freelance digital marketing, I set up a retirement fund and would deposit money into this account as soon as money came my way.

When I obtained my first salary position after I graduated from university, my deposits became automatic. The more I learned about financial freedom, the more I relied on account brokers and financial advisors to help me make smart choices about money.

4 reasons to establish financial connections are . . .

- Obtain and plan realistic savings goals
- Save yourself valuable time with a portfolio manager
- Reduce money-related stress
- Be more objective and stick to the plan

To this day I have deep connections with many financial professionals, including a real estate agent, accountant, teller, and lawyers. I rely on the expertise of others to reach financial goals and freedom. But I give back to those relationships as much as I rely on these individuals by having a positive attitude and sharing my expertise.

Begin a relationship with a financial advisor that not only reassures you but one you thoroughly enjoy working with. Establish a financial connection that gives you a sense of comfort knowing that you are moving towards financial freedom and wellbeing. This connection should also feel uplifting and give you peace of mind.

I did not have the best experience with the first estate lawyer I found to help me through the process of acquiring the Certificate of Estate Trustee Without a Will after Tushar's passing. I had a feeling of low self-esteem after every conversation. It wasn't until I had the thought that not all lawyers earned 80% or higher in their exams that I gave myself permission to find another lawyer. Someone who truly helped me and had clear communication that made me feel empowered. The same can happen for you with your financial relationships.

IMPACT DRIVEN CONNECTIONS

There are going to be days when you don't feel like you are enough. You might start questioning yourself, "What am I doing with my life?" That is why it's important to surround yourself with people who are on the same journey as you with similar passions. If you can grow authentically with them, and express the concerns you are experiencing, they can help you find solutions, share similar concerns, and encourage each other.

Research shows that having impact-driven connections will:

- Increase your sense of belonging and purpose
- Boost your happiness and reduce your stress
- Improve your self-confidence and self-worth
- Encourage you to change or avoid unhealthy lifestyle habits, such as excessive drinking or lack of exercise

You'd be surprised by the number of people who have the same passions as you that also experience the same challenges and trials while pursuing that purpose in life. When you are able to share that similar experience with others, you can create quality relationships by being authentic. You'll obtain quality advice from those that share your passions. In turn, you'll have a surge of momentum from expressing your concerns instead of complaining about being stuck.

I have a network of different groups of people who are on the same journey as me with my mental health initiative, my digital marketing and media initiative, and a different community of thought leaders who are running self-help training. When I don't feel I am on the right path, I can connect with those people who are all on the same page. We offer each other advice, support each other, and ensure each other's continued success.

"People often say that motivation doesn't last. Well, neither does bathing. That's why we recommend it daily."

—**Zig Ziglar,** American author, salesman, and motivational speaker

Reach past your main community of friends and family if they are not supportive and encouraging. They may see your dreams and think they are too big, so they'll discourage you from pursuing them.

Having the right people around you who are impact-driven will help you to move past stumbling blocks because they have been in your shoes. Talk with people who have accomplished what you are trying to achieve. You'll receive the best advice in the world to keep on succeeding.

HOBBY CONNECTIONS

Not all of your friends are going to enjoy the same hobbies that you enjoy. You might have one friend who enjoys going to yoga class or spending the day hiking. Or, you might have another friend who loves to sing karaoke.

Having fun hobbies is a part of your mental and social health. Invest time in doing activities that bring you joy and be willing to have certain people in your network that enjoy the same things. You'll be able to socialize while blowing off some steam or creating something that you can be proud of. You're creating memories with friends and strengthening those connections.

It may sound obvious, but sharing interests is very important for solid friendships. Back in 2010, researchers looked into people's Facebook habits to try and work out why this is.

The study published in the Journal of the Royal Society Interface concluded that we change friends throughout our lives because we form friendships through similarities in our professions, interests, hobbies, religion, or political affiliation.

It's important to spend time on hobbies, but don't try to convince one of your friends to join you if that is not something they enjoy. While I enjoy rock climbing, I have a friend who instead likes to create with her hands. So, we both enjoy attending pottery classes. It brings us both joy. Therefore, I wouldn't bug her about coming to a rock-climbing class with me. Just because I enjoy it doesn't mean all my friends do.

Make time for hobbies with your friends by . . .

- Planning time into your schedule to dedicate to hobbies
- Inviting friends to participate in your hobbies to see who shares the same interests.
- Make it a point to touch base with friends who share the same interests to get feedback on your hobbies and brainstorm new ideas.

If you are still trying to find people to add to your network, be willing to take the first step. Initiate a conversation on social media to connect with others in your field to meet a new mentor. The key to creating new connections is by first offering them something. Then they will be more receptive to offering their knowledge and wisdom. Think about what you could offer to someone you'd love to make a connection with before you take that first step. Always be willing to serve.

In a 2013 study published by The Royal Society, Dunbar stated that the more people we know, the more cognitive load is required of us. Since our brain capacity is limited, maintaining relationships with more than 150 individuals is not only unrealistic but also bordering on impossible. Therefore, we should invest time into each of these relationships that help us stay on track and are in alignment with our life purpose, vision, and goals (You will learn how to define these in Strategy 5).

"Be genuinely interested in everyone you meet and everyone you meet will be genuinely interested in you."

—**Rasheed Ogunlaru,** Author, life and corporate coach

Activity 4: Relationship Improvement

Take this time to review the Wheel of Wellbeing to reflect on your current relationship status. Which one is lacking? What can you improve? Pick three relationships you can commit to improving in the next four weeks.

Social / Personal connections:

____

____

Professional connections:

____

____

Health connections:

____

____

Spiritual connections:

____

____

Financial connections:

____

____

Impact creating / charity / giving back connections:

____

____

Extracurricular activities / hobbies / fun connections:

____

____

"You do not need a certain number of friends, just a number of friends you can be certain of."

—**Itzik Amiel,** Speaker, entrepreneur, author of *The Attention Switch*

PART TWO

Improve Your Chances For Ongoing Success and Wellbeing

Strategy 5. Strengthen Your Mindset

"There are only two ways to live your life. One is as though nothing is a miracle. The other is as though everything is a miracle."

—**Albert Einstein,** German theoretical physicist

Every day there are countless thoughts and messages that are fighting to get your attention. If it wasn't for the Reticular Activating System (RAS), we would have a hard time deciding which thoughts were the most important to focus on at any given point. This part of our brain is rather interesting because it also controls the ability to fall asleep, wake up, and also our fight-or-flight response.

Science Direct has a wonderful collection of medical articles and research studies that dive deep into everything the RAS is responsible for in the brain. One such article is *Governing Principles of Brain Activity* by Edgar Garcia-Rill Ph.D., which states that the RAS, "serves to help us respond to the world around us."

RAS is a network of neurons in the brainstem that trigger the hypothalamus in order to determine behavior and emotion. It then in turn stimulates the prefrontal cortex with a corresponding thought. This is why thoughts and feelings are so closely connected, and why just a thought can trigger a certain emotion inside of us.

The function of RAS is what makes the Law of Attraction

so powerful. Have you ever thought about buying a red jacket and walked down the street to notice all the people wearing red jackets? It didn't just appear. There were people wearing that red jacket all along. You just started paying attention to the color red because you told yourself that you wanted to get a red jacket. The RAS filtered out unimportant messages your brain is receiving on an overload and brought forth only important messages to you.

Whatever we focus our minds on eventually forms into reality. If you spend your days worrying about the future, you'll discover more things to worry about. This is why having a strong mindset is important to improve your chances for success and wellbeing.

Having your purpose statement written out gives your life direction. It is your WHY statement. By clearly outlining your purpose statement and reviewing it daily, you begin to focus your mind on it and find more opportunities to live in accordance with this purpose.

Remember, your purpose statement is not set in stone. A purpose statement can change because of external circumstances that happen like a loss of a loved one or relationship or losing your job. While these can be devastating moments, they can also help you in recreating your life starting with a new purpose statement. It's about living in tune with what you want to do with your life.

Below you'll have space to write your purpose statement again from the previous chapter or adjust it based on the changes you are currently experiencing. From there, we'll go deeper into the Success Roadmap—setting a vision, defining measurable goals, and creating affirmations for each of those goals. (see FIG. 1 below)

My purpose statement is:

____

____

____

____

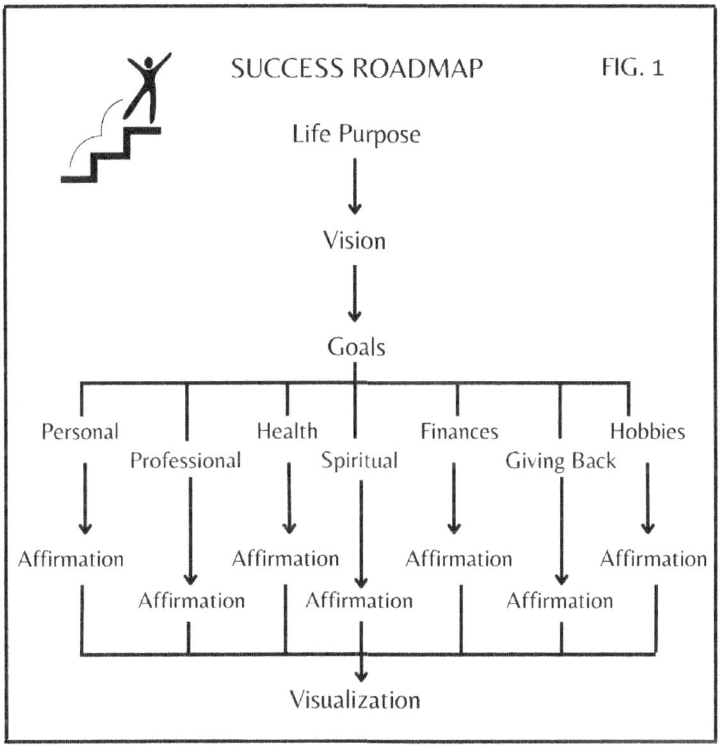

DEFINE A VISION

"If you don't know where you are going, you will probably end up somewhere else."

—**Lawrence J. Peter,** Canadian educator and hierarchy ologist

Now that you have discovered your life purpose statement, your WHY statement, it's time to focus on the WHAT. It's time to clearly define what you want to accomplish by defining a vision.

A vision gives you direction and ensures you are living on track with your purpose.

Without a clear vision, you often get stuck, feel lost, anxious, or unsure. You may be working very hard but perhaps you are working endlessly with no guidance. You haven't taken the time to determine what you are working towards. You may know that your purpose is to be of service and carry humanity forward. But what is it that you want to accomplish to serve your purpose?

My older brother was the diamond of the family. He could ace his tests without needing to study. I believe it was because he took notes during class and reviewed them regularly. He was good at everything—academia, sports, and everyone's favorite. His vision was to attend University of Toronto after he graduated high school. For our family, that would have been a huge win back then.

When he passed away from cerebral malaria during his final year of school, I felt a shift from within. Without announcing it to any of my friends and family, I remained silent as I started to prioritize my grades. I now had a vision of moving to Canada to attend University of Toronto to honor my brother. But in order to do that, I needed to get good grades.

I wrote my vision down on the back of my closet. Every time I would open the door, there it was. I was seeing it each day to gain the motivation needed to start taking action. It began with breaking down my schedule on the back of my notebooks, to planning out every minute of my day for schoolwork, studying, socializing, recreation time, and time to spend with my parents and twin brother. Then I would scratch the schedule out so no one would see them. I didn't want to come across like a loser who is scheduling their entire day at the age of 13.

My older brother had scored a 94% on the CBSE board. CBSE refers to the Central Board of Secondary Education, a national level board of education in India for public and private schools managed by the Government of India. Our question papers were shipped to Lagos, Nigeria and all our answer sheets were shipped back to India for evaluation.

My purpose became to make my parents proud. My vision became that I wanted to score a 90% when I entered 12th grade. I wanted this score so badly that I focused on my vision, wrote down action steps, and had a plan for every minute of the day.

When I received my score at the end of that year, I was not upset that I scored an 89%. After all, that was still an improvement from my last score. What I was also able to accomplish since I was focusing hard on my studies was that I topped the Commerce section with the highest in both English and physical education. As I shifted my mindset to accomplishing my goal, along the way I excelled in other aspects of education. The best part was being accepted to the University of Toronto, making the big move to Canada, and that feeling of making my big brother proud.

To live your purpose, you need a vision of what you want to accomplish in the future. It gives you direction to move and helps with pushing through hurdles when they appear. We all will face challenges. In fact, if you are not being faced with roadblocks, your vision is probably not big enough.

TIP: Picture it clear in your mind. Hold your vision in your mind as often as you can remember, including writing it down so you see it every day. By doing so, you activate the RAS in your brain and begin to focus your mindset on your vision. It's not just a passing thought that comes and goes, but something that shows up in your mind several times a day and activates the RAS to keep you motivated. The more you focus on it, the better you'll be able to clearly define your vision.

Activity 5.1: Define Your Vision

I learned this method of defining a vision from The Young Entrepreneur Council:

A few questions to help you become clear on your vision:

1. Identify what is important to you.

____

2. What do you want to experience?

____

3. Who do you want to be around?

____

4. What steps will you need to take?

____

Now take the time to define your 1–year vision as a way to acknowledge your purpose.

Example: *My vision is to publish a self-help book to help people achieve ongoing success and wellbeing.*

____

____

____

____

EXPERIENCE THE POWER OF GOAL SETTING

"The trouble with not having a goal is that you can spend your life running up and down the field and never score."

—**Bill Copeland,** American poet, writer, and historian

After you have decided WHAT your vision is, the next step is to decide HOW you will accomplish your WHY and WHAT. Some of you may already be familiar with this concept, but perhaps not reaping the benefits from it. Or, you're discouraged and perhaps don't believe in it. Some of you may have never heard or practiced goal setting in your life.

I have been a child of personal development all my life and continue to be. I have been teaching these concepts in my trainings and I always get those people who say, "Why was this not taught to us in school?" Today I want to share simple ways to set goals to move forward and achieve ongoing success and wellbeing. I have learned these concepts from years of studying motivational philosophers, self-help experts, and business coaches—like Zig Ziglar, Tony Robbins, Jack Canfield, Bob Proctor, Brian Tracy, and many more industry leaders. I hope you are as excited as I am for yourself.

When I ask people I meet at social events if they set goals, some of them say, "Yes, of course I do." And when I ask them what their vision is, it throws them off. I have noticed people create goals without a destination in mind. Goals are meant to help us achieve our vision. Without keeping this ultimate vision in mind, we may find ourselves overworking, but not achieving fulfillment. For every vision, you must create 7 goals that will help you sustain success and wellbeing.

Hold on. You might think this is too much.

If you are anything like me and you want to thrive not just survive, you must take the time to write down one goal for the Wheel of Wellbeing—Personal, Professional, Health, Spiritual,

Finances, Giving Back, and Hobbies. We live in a technology-driven fast-paced life. We are constantly being pulled in different directions.

In order to thrive in today's day and age, it's crucial to realize that there are many aspects of wellbeing—not just your career or family. If you focus on just one or two, the others may suffer, and you may find yourself unhappy or even depressed. What is depression? Often when you are suppressing emotions. You are not taking the time to express what you want. Perhaps you can't put a pin on what's missing.

Before we go through an exercise together to help you gain clarity, you may be wondering how to set an effective goal. Here are some guidelines to help you get started:

1. **Set time aside to brainstorm–**
   We often jump right into something before reflecting or creating an outline. Take 5–10 minutes to think about each of the below areas of wellbeing and how your goal will help you progressively move in the direction of your ultimate vision.
2. **Be excited while drafting your goals–**
   I truly believe the energy you bring to the table reflects on your work and your outcomes. Show up with positive and exciting energy. This is your future, but the journey is what makes getting to the top worth it. While drafting your goals, put yourself in a good state of mind. Put on some positive and empowering songs. Perhaps dim the light a little and put on some candles. Dance a little. Sing a little loud.
3. **Set SMART goals–**
   After you have brainstormed a number of goals with good energy, it's time to refine them. This means each goal should be—Specific, Measurable, Achievable, Realistic, and Timely. Determining SMART goals will help you stay in control of your outcome and

keep you accountable, motivated, and focused. My mentor, Jack Canfield, always says, "How much? By when?" Breaking down your goal this way gives you the ability to track your progress and celebrate your successes.

Some of you may see the word 'achievable' in SMART and decide to shrink. But if you are going to spend the energy on dreaming, may as well dream a little big so that it makes you grow. Pushes you to expand. Perhaps you may need to learn a new process. Or, you want to change your current habits so in turn, you have to create a new routine or learn a new skill. Network with a different group of people.

Setting clear deadlines that are reasonable sets a strong purpose, intention and makes the goal more concrete. You have increased motivation for getting it done and then celebrating the small wins.

For example:

NO: To obtain a new skill set in three months.

YES: To learn to bake a red velvet cake by July 5th, 2022, at 7:00 pm eastern time.

By creating specific deadlines, you're setting your goal concrete. It won't be able to slip away or be set on the back burner.

4. **Review your goal daily–**
   You want to write, read, or say it out loud daily. It will help you build up feelings of anticipation, excitement, and motivation to help you keep reaching for your clear goal with measurable action steps. It will be at the forefront of your mind because you've deemed it important. Reviewing it daily activates the RAS in your brain to focus your prefrontal cortex to be on the lookout for opportunities or resources.

Activity 5.2: Set Smart Goals

Keeping the 1–year vision you drafted in front of you. Now it's time to create 1–year goals to help you achieve your vision under each of these areas of wellbeing.

Area	Goal
1. Personal	______________________
2. Professional	______________________
3. Health	______________________
4. Spiritual	______________________
5. Finances	______________________
6. Giving Back	______________________
7. Hobbies	______________________

CREATING EFFECTIVE AFFIRMATIONS

"Affirmations are your mental vitamins, providing the supplementary positive thoughts we need to balance the barrage of negative events and thoughts we experience daily."

—**Tia Walker,** Journalist and professional blogger

Affirmations are more than just positive statements. They are statements that describe your goals as if they are already complete. As if you have achieved that goal. It is in the present. You are living it. While you could use scripted affirmations that are motivational and inspiring, creating affirmations that are based on your specific goals will have a more powerful effect. I urge you to create unique affirmations for each of your goals.

If you believe affirmations don't work, it is probably because you haven't been using them correctly. It's not magic. It's science. It retrains our brain by creating neural pathways to keep us goal-oriented, focused, and motivated. We now have several neuroscientific studies that show changes in the brain that were visible through magnetic resonance imaging (MRI) scans.

Did you know our mind cannot differentiate the real from fantasy? So, when we believe something is real for us, our external actions align with it. A study done by the Annenberg School of Communication in collaboration with researchers at the University of Michigan and UCLA shows that people who practice affirmations every morning have increased activity in the medial prefrontal cortex (MPFC). This is the part of the brain that takes control over intrinsic activity, bringing in changes inside your body.

The study also showed that affirmations have shown to dampen pain and help maintain balance in the face of threats. Affirmations also activate the ventral striatum and ventromedial prefrontal cortex, which are reward centers of the brain that respond to pleasurable experiences like publishing a book, getting your exercise done for the day, or eating your favorite ice cream. Which is the reason why a person practicing self-affirmations could feel full of self-confidence and good thoughts. So, the next time you are filled with negative thoughts, try replacing them with more positive ones.

Affirmations are scientifically proven as a method for self-improvement because of their ability to rewire our brains. They direct our brain to form new clusters of 'positive thought' neurons. This is why they play an integral role by breaking patterns of the ANTs in our brain (Automatic Negative Thoughts) to become automatic positive thoughts.

In an article written by a head and neck surgeon, Rohini Radhakrishnan published on *Medicine Net*, she suggests repeating the affirmations every day for at least 5–10 minutes, preferably out loud with energy and enthusiasm.

Here are some guidelines on creating effective affirmations suggested by so many industry-leading experts and professionals like Dr. Rohini Radhakrishnan, my mentor Jack Canfield, Bob Proctor, and so many more:

1. Begin with the words 'I am', as they are extremely powerful words that act as a command for your mind to make happen.

2. Use the present tense. Write it and say it as if it is already here at this moment. You have achieved it.

3. State it positively and do not affirm what you don't want.

4. Keep it simple, brief, and specific. If your affirmations are vague, so will your outcomes.

5. Include gratitude or a feeling word. This one I learned from Bob Proctor, 'I am now happy and grateful that . . .' This already puts you in a positive vibration that is necessary to attract more good.

6. Create affirmations about yourself, not others. You cannot control other people's thoughts or behaviors. You only have control over your own.

In order to improve your chances of ongoing success and wellbeing, practice affirmations daily. One of the affirmations I recently created was, "I am so happy and grateful that my book 'Ongoing Success and Wellbeing' hit #1 bestseller on Amazon." See how specific this affirmation is? It contains the traditional "I am . . ." statement coupled with emotion and the specific details of my measurable goal.

When I made the decision to switch over from coffee and move over to juicing celery, I struggled in the beginning because I didn't like the taste at all. I created an affirmation that, "I am so happy and grateful for drinking celery juice every morning because I am loving the taste." I would tell everyone about it. Now I crave celery juice every morning and sometimes have it in the evening.

Here are additional examples of affirmations:

- I am so happy and grateful now that money is coming to me in increasing amounts through 3 sources on a continuous basis.
- I am happy driving my new red Ferrari 458 Italia car.
- I am enjoying living in my new beach house in San Diego.
- I am confident socially and enjoy meeting new people at networking events.
- I am so happy and grateful that I have reached my ideal weight of 150 pounds.
- I am enjoying the thrill of hiking.
- I am so happy and grateful that I am now enjoying my relationship with my father.

Now, let's dive into creating an affirmation for each of your goals.

Activity 5.3: Affirmations

Based on the purpose, vision, and goal you've written in this strategy, take the time to write an affirmation for that goal. Remember to create 'I am . . .' statements that contain emotion and a '–ing' word.

Area	Goal	Affirmation
1. Personal	______________	______________
2. Professional	______________	______________
3. Health	______________	______________
4. Spiritual	______________	______________
5. Finances	______________	______________
6. Giving Back	______________	______________
7. Hobbies	______________	______________

VISUALIZATION

"Visualization is daydreaming with a purpose."

—**Bo Bennett,** Author, host, and producer

Visualization is the practice of picturing your future vision as reality. The most successful people for decades have practiced this strategy of visualizing their desired outcomes to create new levels of motivation, excitement, and inspiration. Visualization also activates the RAS filter in your brain to bring resources or opportunities to your awareness that will help you achieve your desired outcome. It programs the subconscious mind to work when you are sleeping, eating, bathing, walking, meeting friends, or networking. It is always working for you. Remember to work on the tool first.

I use this strategy all the time. For example, before I go up on stage to deliver a talk, I close my eyes and picture how the audience is feeling. I visualize some people being moved by my message, having transformations, having their breakthroughs—the audience is engaging with me and fully present. They are asking me questions and are excited to implement strategies that I share with them. When I open my eyes, I feel less nervous and more confident in delivering that talk. I feel increased energy and excitement to create an impact on people's lives. After all, it's not about me but the audience coming out to improve themselves.

Before I started writing this book, I drafted my vision, goals, affirmations, and then I wrote a full page of how I see this book has transformed people's lives and given them hope. I felt the impact from the book and the opportunities that came my way. I won't bore you with the details, but I am hoping you feel the change internally as you keep reading this book one chapter at a time daily.

To begin visualizing, I want to invite you to sit in a comfortable place where you won't be distracted. Perhaps play some light meditative music like Tibetan singing bowls. Close your eyes and be still. Now bring to your awareness one of the areas of life and the subsequent goals. Visualize it has been achieved. If one of your health goals was to improve your mental health.

Think about what it feels like when you have achieved it? Who are you celebrating with? Who are the people that are around you? What are they saying to you? What does that success look like? What are the benefits you are reaping from having achieved this goal? Is there any food around? What does the room you are all in smell like? What kind of house are you in? Include as many details as possible when you are visualizing your goal to create that sense of reality now instead of what is going to happen in the future. It is happening right now when you are visualizing the end result.

Now, write down what you were able to create in your mind in the exercise at the end of this chapter.

3–2 TO BE TO DO LIST

"The only impossible journey is the one you never begin."

—**Tony Robbins,** American author, coach, speaker, and philanthropist

The reality of your vision will only come to fruition when you take action daily. This goes back to my **3–2 rule** that I practice every day. After I focus on three things for my wellbeing, I focus on completing two action steps towards my goal. When you are visualizing your goal, you'll gain inspiration and motivation to take action.

After you finish your visualization session, start writing down a list to-do list. Of your list, which two can you accomplish today? It's important to think of action steps that are obtainable. You don't want to create an action step that is unrealistic.

For example, if your goal is to obtain your first public speaking event in 3 months on the dot, an action step might be reaching out to different company leaders that meet your target audience. Your to-do step can be deciding which leaders you're going to contact, followed by which one you're going to contact first. That's two steps right there that can be accomplished today.

An unrealistic action step would be cold calling different CEOs and top leaders without having practiced your pitch or defining your purpose statement. Though there is nothing wrong with cold calls, this is a to-do step that requires preparation and intention. Therefore, if you start calling around without preparing, you set yourself up for failure. This is the type of failure that you'll learn from by understanding what your first step should have been.

No matter how big your dreams are, remember to take to-be

to-do steps each day. Start small and manageable, and as your confidence grows, take leaps of faith and large steps towards ongoing success and wellbeing. Remember, "If not me, then who?" You got this!

"Action is the foundational key to all success."

—**Pablo Picasso**, Spanish painter, sculptor, printmaker, ceramicist, and theater designer

Activity 5.4: Visualize

What does it look like to achieve my goal?

Activity 5.5:
To-Be To-Do List

What are the 3–2 steps you will implement today?

#1 ______________________________ (Wellbeing)

#2 ______________________________ (Wellbeing)

#3 ______________________________ (Wellbeing)

#4 ______________________________ (Goal)

#5 ______________________________ (Goal)

"A good plan today is better than a perfect plan tomorrow."

—**George Patton,** General in the United States Army

Strategy 6. Have an Attitude of Gratitude

"Gratitude turns what we have into enough, and more. It turns denial into acceptance, chaos into order, confusion into clarity."

—**Melody Beattie,** American author of self-help books

About a month before my twin brother was released from this life, we went on a cruise together. It was a time to rest and relax, to enjoy the sights, and spend time together. I was standing along the balcony of the cruise ship, looking out over the waves and feeling the wind on my face, when my brother asked me, "What do you like about me?"

The question surprised me, and even more shocking was the fact that I couldn't think of anything. "How can I not think of anything?" I thought before I blurted out the first thing that came to mind. The immediate response was not genuine, so I flipped the script on him.

"What do you like about your girlfriend?" I asked, wanting to take the pressure off of me. He continued to list all the things he liked about her, and then the conversation turned away from the topic all together.

What this experience taught me is that we shouldn't wait to express our gratitude. As soon as I see what I like about someone, I tell them. This will solidify relationships, create deep connections, and allow you to feel fulfilled with those you invest in. Don't wait till someone passes away to say all the things you like about them.

When you express gratitude to someone, expect nothing else in return. This is the pure nature of gratitude and where the habit of an attitude of gratitude is formed. Give freely of your gratitude that can be verbal acknowledgment or in the form of a gift.

I enjoy seeing the look on someone's face when they unexpectedly receive flowers from a loved one. To see the smile light upon a person's face when they are praised and appreciated for their hard work. To instantly turn someone's day around, express your gratitude towards them. Let them know from the bottom of your heart the things you like about them as soon as the thought enters your mind.

There are a multitude of ways to feel and express gratitude. You can think of your past experiences and feel gratitude towards positive memories, blessings you've experienced, and even childhood experiences. You can think of the people connected to your present moment that you feel fortunate to have in your life. As you think about the future, you can maintain an optimistic outlook that you're going to receive more things to be grateful for.

That's the power of having an attitude of gratitude. The more you appreciate what you have in your life, the more you'll find and discover ways to show your gratitude. From having running water in your home to warm clothes to wear each day, there are plenty of little things to be grateful for. Then there are the big things in life to give thanks for, which include all the people in your network.

Right now, think of all the things that you can be grateful for. All the small things coupled with the major blessings you have in your life. Hold on to that feeling and let it carry you through each day as you cultivate an attitude of gratitude. Always acknowledge the things you are grateful for each day.

BENEFITS OF GRATITUDE GIVING

"Gratitude will shift you to a higher frequency, and you will attract much better things."

—**Rhonda Byrne,** Australian television writer and producer

Through many positive psychology research studies, the state of being grateful and showing gratitude is always tied to the feeling of happiness. When you practice an attitude of gratitude, you will feel more positive emotions. More often than not, you'll consider everyday events to be for your good. You'll even notice an improvement in your health.

One of the biggest benefits of being mindful of all the things you can be grateful for each day is having a higher probability of defeating unexpected obstacles and challenges. Even when you have experienced one of the worst days in your life, with an optimistic mindset, you can deal with the situation and still have the clarity to choose your response.

One study conducted by Dr. Robert A. Emmons and Dr. Michael E. McCullough showcased the powerful benefits of gratitude. For a 10-week period, they had three groups focus on writing sentences each week on a particular topic. One group was assigned to write things they were grateful for, while another was tasked with writing about things that irritated them. The final group was simply asked to write down events that affected them.

Those who focused on the things that they were grateful for each week became more optimistic and felt better about their lives. In addition, they also exercised more and had fewer trips to see a doctor.

Can you imagine the benefits in your life when you seek out all the things you are grateful for? Whether you do this every day or once a week, take the time to write them down. Spend a moment before going to bed each night to think of all the things you can be grateful for and to express gratitude to your friends and family before the day is through.

Positive Psychology lists some benefits of gratitude to help you get excited about creating a new routine of giving thanks. They include:

- Increases psychological wellbeing.
- Increases self-esteem.
- Improves our friendships.
- Increases social support.
- Makes us more optimistic.
- Shows reduction of materialism.
- Reduces impatience and improves decision-making.

WAYS TO CULTIVATE GRATITUDE

"When I started counting my blessings, my whole life turned around."

—**Willie Nelson,** American musician, actor, and activist

The art of being grateful is a way for everyone to become more aware of appreciating what they have instead of always looking for something new to fulfill them. Sometimes we feel unhappy, so we try to replace that feeling with a fresh experience, purchase, or shift in our career. Instead, true happiness comes from appreciating what you have *now*.

I was so grateful for my first big job in a sales environment. I learned I had resilience. Even though I couldn't make sales in the first five months, I was grateful. I started to go above and beyond, to find more things for being grateful and having a good work ethic. I was the first in the office; I stayed later and took on new roles. I did all of this because I wanted to add value, learn more and express my gratitude for them believing in me.

It was a harsh working atmosphere filled with macho men,

competition, and the overall idea from my coworkers that a woman could not excel in this type of sales role. Instead of focusing on all the negative attitudes from my coworkers who liked to complain about everything in the office, including the boss, I focused on every little thing I could be grateful for.

I would show my attitude of gratitude every day despite the stressful situation. I would thank my coworkers when they would teach me something new. Daily I would remind myself of all the new opportunities that I was thankful for. Even my boss, who was very hard to get along with, I would appreciate him as well.

The more I focused on this mindset instead of what my coworkers were complaining about, I was able to flourish in that sales environment. No one thought I would make it as a woman, but I wasn't concerned about what others thought. I was only focused on what I thought about myself and the many things I could be grateful for.

I helped the company break even before I left. I found out that they still have the same salary after three years of progress. This taught me to always be grateful, but never content. There is always an enormous benefit in trying out different roles to find your true potential.

If you want to cultivate gratitude regularly, consider writing someone a thank-you note. Nurture the relationships you have with others by expressing your appreciation of that person's impact on your life. Put that letter in the mail or deliver it yourself. As you begin this practice, try to write one every month, and include yourself on that list of people to write a thank-you note to.

Keep a journal of all the things that you are grateful for each day. You can keep it beside your bed as a reminder to reflect on gratitude before falling asleep, or you can make it a part of your morning routine. It can even be a pleasant ritual as soon as you get home to create a pause in your day to unwind and refocus your mindset on the positive. It makes a splendid book to look back on at the end of the year.

There are many ways to count your blessings. This can be

done through prayer if you are religious. Or you can practice mindful meditation where you focus on the present moment without judging yourself or the events of the day. Blessings can be the warmth of the sun on your skin or just enjoying listening to the birds sing.

Emmons and McCullough's (2003) work was groundbreaking and has set the stage for much of the research on gratitude that has been conducted since it was published.

Their article, titled "Counting blessings versus burdens: An experimental investigation of gratitude and subjective wellbeing in daily life," describes three studies conducted to explore the potential emotional and interpersonal benefits of gratitude.

Study 1

Study 1 involved a group of around 200 undergraduate students, split into one gratitude group, one "hassles" group, and one neutral control group. The gratitude group received instructions to think back over their past week and write down up to five things they were grateful for in their life. The hassles group was instructed to write up to five hassles or irritants they had experienced over the past week. The control group showed up to five events that impacted them over the last week.

The students completed these "weekly reports" for 10 weeks, along with items assessing wellbeing, physical symptoms, reactions to aid or help-giving, and appraisals of their overall state. Results from this study showed that participants in the gratitude group felt better about their life on the whole, more optimistic about the upcoming week, and reported fewer physical complaints than participants in the other groups.

Study 2

In study 2, a sample of about 160 undergraduate students in a health psychology class completed 16 "daily experience rating forms." These rating forms were nearly identical to the forms from study 1 but referenced the daily time period instead of the previous weekly time period. The first two groups were also given the gratitude and hassles instructions, respectively, but the third group was instructed to write about the ways in which they were better off than others. This was dubbed the "downward social comparison" group.

Participants also indicated the frequency with which they exercised, the number of hours of sleep they got the previous night, and whether they had engaged in pro-social behaviors each day.

Results from study 2 showed that those in the gratitude group reported greater positive affect and more pro-social behavior than participants in the other groups, although there was no significant difference found in the frequency of exercise or amount of sleep.

Study 3

Study 3 was conducted with a group of adults who suffered from a neuromuscular disease. They completed a packet of 21 daily experience rating forms similar to those employed in study 2. Participants were assigned to either the gratitude group, where they were given the same instructions as the gratitude group in the previous studies and completed measures of daily affect, wellbeing, and other health and daily living activities, or the control group, in which participants completed only the measured portion of the daily tasks.

The findings from study 3 showed that those in the gratitude condition reported increased **subjective wellbeing**, greater positive affect, and more hours of quality sleep. Ratings from the participants' significant others confirmed that there was a noticeable difference in their wellbeing as well.

These three studies provided evidence that gratitude can have a significant impact on an individual's emotional, mental, and possibly even physical state. While there had been other explorations of gratitude as a psychological construct, this was one of the first articles suggesting that the benefits of gratitude may be far greater than we realized at the time.

If you remember anything about this article, remember this: Emmons and McCullough (2003) showed that counting your blessings seems to be a much more effective way of enhancing your quality of life than counting your burdens.

Every day presents a plethora of things to be grateful for. As you start this new practice, focus on all the small things from good food to enjoying music in the car on the way to and from work. From there, go big! As you reflect on all that you are grateful for each day, don't forget those that you interact with. Be willing to let them know that you appreciate them. Remember to be specific so you can really show that you are genuine with your attitude of gratitude.

"Life is what we make it, always has been, always will be."

—Grandma Moses

Activity 6: Today I Am Grateful For

There are seven main environments in which we spend our time that you've seen in the Wheel of Wellbeing. They include personal life, professional life, health, spirituality, finances, giving back, and hobbies. Take the time now to reflect on these different environments and what you can be thankful for today.

Today I am grateful for . . .

1. Personal life ______________________________
2. Professional life ______________________________
3. Health ______________________________
4. Spiritual ______________________________
5. Financial ______________________________
6. Giving back ______________________________
7. Hobbies ______________________________

"Gratitude is riches. Complaint is poverty."

—**Doris Day,** American actress, singer, and animal welfare activist

Strategy 7. The Future is Skills-Based. Not Gender-Based.

"Never chase opportunities. Let it come to you by creating value and building rare skill sets."

—**Johannes Larrson,** Swedish entrepreneur and affiliate marketing expert

Your intuition is the guiding force in your life, having whispered that you need to experience a change in order to obtain the desired outcome you want. But the truth of the matter is that *you* are the change. Any change you want to experience first starts with you.

Long gone are the days when men are the primary breadwinners. Being the only saleswoman for an Ad Tech company that was making millions a month forced me to take action. I had to develop my skills on the job because there were certain things that university did not prepare me for.

I spent a month doing everything I could to add value to my work environment and take coworkers to the next level. I enjoyed finding loopholes and capturing any money for the company that had slipped through the cracks. After three months of improving, I then asked for my own accounts to manage.

For the next seven months, I developed all the accounts in Europe because no one wanted to work those hours. I started earning commission after the first month. After the first year of working 2 roles, I went to the owner to reveal everything.

I showed the owner of the company the full list of clients I had been managing and the revenue the company had made because of my efforts. The owner was so shocked that he couldn't say no to me.

At the beginning of that career, I didn't know how to cold-call CEOs and use their lingo. Developing the skills I needed to become successful helped me reach that desired level in the company. I would walk around the office taking lots of notes. I went to everyone and asked them about their job and challenges to learn their role.

The main point of this story is that your success is all on you. To improve your chances of success, you need to develop the skill set that will take you into the future. It has nothing to do with gender, but the amount of effort you're willing to put in.

With all of my additional skill sets, I left that company to develop my own digital media agency. I never imagined owning my own business, but all of my experience and new skills showed me how possible it was. Now I manage VASH media, a successful company because of the skills I had developed in the past.

All we need to do is improve our own skills to ensure a future of success. You can never be content with your current situation. The first step is deciding that you are going to learn a new skill set. Have that vision and set it into a measurable goal. It all goes back to your purpose statement, how you want to serve others, and the skills you're going to need to make it a reality. You have the power to shape your future by deciding what new skills you need to have in your toolbox.

CONSTANTLY IMPROVING SKILL SET

Susan B. Anthony believed that failure was impossible. Thanks to this New York disrupter, she is one of the main reasons women get to collect stickers on election days in the United States.

Anna Bissell became CEO of her husband's vacuum company after his passing. She was the first female CEO in America, using aggressive marketing, landing deals with major retailers, and taking the brand internationally. She was also one of the first to offer workers' pension plans and compensation for injuries.

Elizabeth Blackwell didn't consider becoming a doctor till a friend explained her medical treatment would have been easier if her doctor was a woman. She was inspired to change the world, becoming the first woman in America to receive her medical degree from New York's Geneva Medical College. She later helped found the New York Infirmary for Women and Children and was a professor at the London School of Medicine for Women.

None of these women leaders who pioneered a way for others to follow were born with the skill set needed to be successful. They had to learn by first trying. They had to constantly improve their skill set, preparing them for new opportunities. What helped them to reach new heights was always learning and constantly adding to their wealth of knowledge.

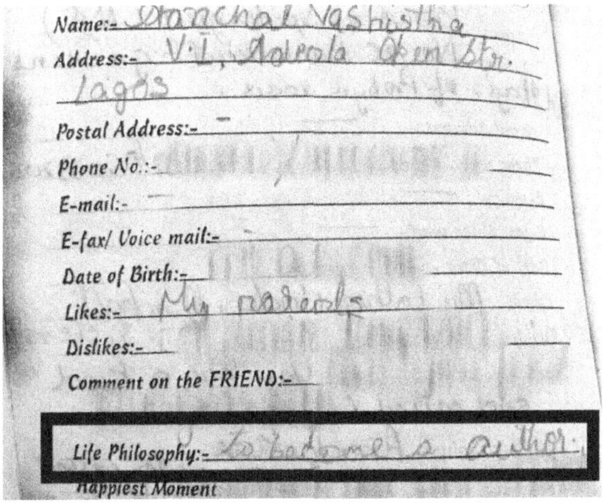
Name:-
Address:-
Lagos
Postal Address:-
Phone No.:-
E-mail:-
E-fax/ Voice mail:-
Date of Birth:-
Likes:-
Dislikes:-
Comment on the FRIEND:-
Life Philosophy:-
Happiest Moment

If you are a man or woman stuck in a situation you're not happy in, then it's time to learn a new skill set. Whatever you want to be, write it down. Then, discover what skill set you need to accomplish that dream. You are discovering how entrepreneurs have a lifetime of success. By always learning new skills.

When I was in the 6th grade, I wrote in my friend's slam book, a book that contained a collection of inspirational messages from friends, that I wanted to be an author. Recently, I had the opportunity to meet up with this friend in California and he showed me his slam book. There it was in black and white. My goal to become an author never changed. Just my focus as I searched for my passion and purpose.

HOW TO MASTER A NEW SKILL

In today's business environment, mastering a new skill set is no longer an option. Being able to learn new skills is one key to success. You need to be on the lookout for new opportunities that will stretch you, make you feel uncomfortable, and teach you what it takes to go further than what most would consider impossible. This is something that should be continually happening and not a once-a-year occurrence.

Whether you want to become a public speaker, learn to use social media, or analyze data, determine the steps that are going to help you learn this new skill set and master it. Go behind learning a new task or job. You also want to become an expert as well.

Michael Daws, a writer for LifeHack, describes five ways to master a new skill set:

1. **Deconstruct the skill and make it less overwhelming–** Most skill mastery is built upon learning a bunch of skills put together. Break it down into sections so you don't overwhelm yourself with trying to do it all at once.

2. **Commit yourself to 20 hours of practice–** This is the entire focus in Josh Kaufman's "The First 20 Hours: How To Learn Anything . . . Fast". Before you

learn something new, set a goal point that you would like to reach, and write a schedule and stick to it.

3. **Define what it means to you to 'master' the skill–** One person's definition of mastering a skill may be significantly different from yours. Decide what it truly means to master a new skill set and then set your goals around that definition.
4. **Imagine yourself doing the skill–** Make it a habit to visualize yourself performing your new skill. It will boost your morale and help you feel more confident that you can master the skill exactly how you want to.
5. **Be confident but be humble–** Once you practice the new skill set, act as though you've been doing it for years. This will boost your confidence and make learning go a lot better, but don't let it get to your head.

Determine how much time and energy you can dedicate to learning a new skill. While some might believe that if you have to work hard at something, it means you lack ability, instead realize that learning a new skill takes commitment and hard work. Unless you're prepared to work hard, you won't get very far. Commit to the new skill you want to learn and make the time for it, just like any other measurable goal.

When thinking of a new skill you want to learn, ensure that the skill applies to your career or the career you'd like to have. Gaining a new skill is an investment to your future. You need to know upfront what the return will be.

"I am not a product of my circumstances. I am a product of my decisions."

—**Stephen Covey,** American educator, author, and speaker

It's also important to know how you learn best. While some can learn from reading, others need live demonstrations to understand new material. Gaining that 'hands-on' experience and sharing your journey with others makes for impactful learning. Identify the best learning environment you'll thrive in before you get started so you don't waste your time struggling to learn a new skill set.

On this journey to routinely improve your skill set, start small. Self-improvement can seem overwhelming, and that's why this book is best digested by one strategy a day. If you try to take on everything, you'll never do it. Focus on one skill set at a time and break that down into manageable goals. If you want to become a public speaker, begin by speaking up in meetings within the first five minutes. Take the time to reflect on getting the right help by working with those that already possess the skill set you are trying to learn. Take small action steps to reach your overall goal.

To really become an expert with a new skill set, challenge yourself to teach it to others. The best way to learn is to teach, so within six months of developing a new skill, notice those to whom you can teach it to. You'll be surprised by the huge difference you can make in the lives of others by being willing to teach what you know.

Key points to remember:

1. Select a skill that is of value to your current position or the future position you are striving to achieve.
2. Divide the skill into manageable tasks that you can create weekly action steps for.
3. Reflect on what you are learning and how it relates to what you are trying to accomplish.
4. Be willing to ask others for guidance. Remember that success is a team sport.

5. Learning a new skill set takes time. Be committed and willing to work hard.

6. Expect to learn by trial and error. When you first don't succeed, try and try again.

"If you hear a voice within you say, "you cannot paint," then by all means paint and that voice will be silenced."

—**Vincent Van Gogh,** Dutch painter

Activity 7:
Learn A New Skill Set

Keeping in mind your purpose statement and the goals you've already written in this book, what new skills do you need to learn? List them below.

1. Personal life ______________________________
2. Professional life ______________________________
3. Health ______________________________
4. Spiritual ______________________________
5. Financial ______________________________
6. Giving back ______________________________
7. Hobbies ______________________________

Who do you know that can help you learn one of these new skill sets? Or where can you go to start learning or sign up for a class?

Strategy 8. Overcome Troubling and Difficult Events

"Everything you've ever wanted is on the other side of fear."

—**George Addair,** Real estate developer, and author of *Post-Civil War Atlanta*

The moment you drop the ball, or the world seems to be falling apart, you're going to feel a moment of distress. Your mind will race to find a solution, your heart is going to beat hard in your chest, and you'll feel your palms start to sweat. It's a moment you'll never forget, but also a moment that is time-limited.

Being in distress doesn't last forever. You don't want to make any big decisions during a temporary period of fear or anger. Therefore, take the time to acknowledge yourself, how you are feeling, and the desired outcome you want in that moment of distress. Recognize that pain and suffering, and then weigh your decisions. Do it for yourself.

Take ownership of the situation despite the overwhelming event that has just landed on your plate. This is how you overcome troubling and difficult moments in your life by choosing your response and how you'll react to set yourself up for ongoing success and wellbeing.

"Try and fail, but never fail to try."

—**Jared Leto,** American actor and musician

The last time you felt distressed, how did you react? Were you quick to anger and lash out? Did you cut someone out of your life? Did it take days to recover from the grief and initial shock?

As you think about the answers to those questions, did those responses lead to the outcome you might have preferred to experience?

Powerful emotions of grief and sorrow cause us to react quickly, like being bitten by a mosquito, needing to wipe it away and treat the itch. It's *instinct* to want to move as quickly as possible to a place of safety and peace when a troubling event happens.

How can you change your response in a difficult situation to match the outcome that you want? When your boss breaks the news they are laying off a third of the company and you're on that list, what is the desired outcome? Of course, you want to have financial security, so you can choose to spend the rest of the day searching for new jobs or finally commit to going back to school as you've always dreamed of. Every disaster is a chance for success.

ACKNOWLEDGE THE STRESS. FOCUS ON THE SOLUTION.

"Being challenged in life is inevitable, being defeated is optional."

—**Roger Crawford,** Differently abled tennis player, motivational speaker, and author

When difficult situations happen, for they will happen to everyone regularly, it's important to acknowledge that stress. When you suppress negative emotions, that will lead to depression. Therefore, allow yourself to feel those emotions because no emotion is bad. Feeling a wide range of emotions makes us human.

While you acknowledge those negative feelings, remember not to focus on them. Don't let them consume you to where you can't think of a solution or move forward. Remind yourself that this moment of grief and sadness is temporary. So, while your body is feeling the rollercoaster of emotions, let your mind focus on the solution.

It has been five years since I lost my twin brother to suicide. People often ask me, "How did you do it? How do you keep going?" and seem in awe of my strength and perseverance. I miss my twin brother dearly. When there's a win, he's the one person I think about and want to share that moment with. I find myself in those moments, giving myself the permission to cry or dance or just being. I tell myself, "How sorry I am this happened to you and how I will do everything in my power to take care of you. I am with you every step of the way." After a few minutes of creating a safe space to express myself, I clean up, brush off my shoulders and I feel empowered to continue with my 3–2 to-be to-do list.

When you suddenly lose your job, you can find another one that is possibly much better than the one you had before.

When you lose someone close to you suddenly, you can commit to living a more purposeful life in their honor.

When you are diagnosed with an illness that you'll have to battle for the rest of your life, you can make the choice to live life to the fullest instead of letting that one aspect of you hold you back. It is a choice. It's not easy, but it is one that will contribute to your wellbeing and help you in your pursuit of ongoing achievement.

"Obstacles don't have to stop you. If you run into a wall, don't turn around and give up. Figure out how to climb it, go through it, or work around it."

—**Michael Jordan,** Former professional basketball player, and American businessman

The moment the new obstacle has been placed before you or life suddenly happens against your favor, take the time to visualize the feeling of overcoming that challenge. Often it is easy to become overwhelmed with negative emotions. Battle back that feeling with the happiness, peace, and joy you'll feel from discovering the solution to that problem.

Just like distress is temporary, often fading away faster than you can originally imagine, a solution can be discovered just as fast. When you are looking at the problem in front of you, step back and take a break. Visualize the feeling of overcoming the challenge and refocus on those feelings. The longer you spend visualizing the feeling of moving past the obstacle, the sooner a solution will come to mind once you're able to put your mindset into a positive set of feelings. Take a deep breath, remember that this too shall pass, and be prepared to take action as soon as a solution comes to mind.

The American Psychological Association (APA) suggested healthy ways to handle life's stressors:

1. Try to eliminate the stressors.
2. Cultivate social support.
3. Seek good nutrition.
4. Relax your muscles.
5. Meditate.
6. Protect your sleep.
7. Get active.
8. Take a moment in nature.
9. Keep your pleasurable activities going.
10. Reframe your thinking.
11. Seek help.

REACH OUT TOGETHER

Everyone has something they are dealing with right now. You can either see it clearly on their faces, or you have no idea that it even exists. Pretending that life is perfect each day is a fallacy. Instead, acknowledge the troubles you are facing as well as give those around you the opportunity to open up. When you can't find the right solution, it's time to reach out.

Tushar's passing was a hard pill for me to swallow. I started looking for a community of like-minded people with whom I could open up about what I was feeling and to discover good healing strategies. My network at the time did not know how to talk to me or even look at me after the tragedy.

I ended up changing therapists four times until I found the one that worked best for me. The healing process began for me as I fought for my own wellbeing. I stayed consistent and utilized everything that I was learning about mental health and overcoming difficult events. I truly felt that everyone deserves to have access to professional help and self-help support groups.

When I started Reach Out Together, I was hosting events once a month. Though the entire process was new to me, I continued to persevere even when I felt like I had no time for rest. I knew what I was learning through my official certifications and sessions with my own therapist that healing was possible and should be available to everyone.

During the time of your life when you are struggling to overcome troubling situations, seek professional help. Therapists are not just for those who suffer from mental health issues like severe depression and anxiety. We all experience these feelings because life is often unexpected. Therefore, it's normal and healthy to meet with a therapist routinely so that you have someone to open up to about what you've been experiencing. In return, you'll gain an outside perspective and sound advice from someone who is unbiased.

If meeting with a therapist doesn't sound like a doable idea, seek a support group. Work with people you don't know. You can share so much more and become vulnerable. There will always be ups and downs, and when it causes a lot of stress, it's up to you to find the support that is going to help.

This ties back into self-mastery in understanding your likes, dislikes, and what brings you joy. This will help navigate you from that negative place to one that is positive by taking one small action of joy after another.

"Our very survival depends on our ability to stay awake, to adjust to new ideas, to remain vigilant and to face the challenge of change."

—**Martin Luther King Jr.,** Spokesman, activist, and leader in the Civil Rights movement

Activity 8: Give Yourself Permission

Sit, stand, or lay down in a place where you won't be disturbed. A place where you feel safe and are free to express yourself in any way. When you're ready, place your hands over your heart. Close your eyes and take a deep breath.

At this moment, give yourself permission to feel. Acknowledge how you've been feeling and allow yourself to cry if you need to. Express the emotions you've been suppressing.

When you're ready, say to yourself, "I'm so sorry this happened to you. I'm here for you. I'm going to take care of you. I'm never going to leave you."

Stay in this moment for as long as you need to help calm your nerves or any feeling of anxiety. When you come out of this activity, take the time to record your thoughts and feelings.

____

____

____

____

"The battles that count aren't the ones for gold medals. The struggles within yourself—the invisible battles inside all of us—that's where it's at."

—**Jesse Owens,** American track and field athlete

PART THREE

Lock In Discipline For Ongoing Success and Wellbeing

Strategy 9. Self-Motivation

"The one common denominator of all successful people is their hunger to push through their fears."

—**Tony Robbins,** American author, coach, speaker, and philanthropist

Of all the successful people that you know, what do you think is the one thing they all have in common? Are they all really smart? Maybe they are wealthy? The truth is that all successful people have a deep drive that motivates them to succeed each and every time. It depends on how 'hungry' they are to succeed and how well they can focus their mind on their goals.

Self-motivation is the technique you use to encourage yourself to make progress each day towards your goals. You often have to rely on certain techniques when you are faced with a challenge, stumbling block, or wall. Instead of thinking that you *want* to go to the gym today to stay mentally fit, you instead think that you *must* go to the gym today. You turn all of your *wants* into *musts*. It simply becomes non-negotiable.

With all the goals and dreams that you are looking to achieve, you're going to want to reach down deep and find that motivation to keep going every day. While you might have a network of individuals that are cheering you on—it comes down to you to make the change.

One way that I stay motivated is by creating mantras that are unique to my goals. I can say them every morning and throughout the day to not only keep my mind focused on my goal but to give myself the motivation I need to be on the lookout for new opportunities that are going to bring me closer to living by my purpose statement.

It's important to note that what motivates me will not necessarily motivate you. Everyone is different and what works for me is not going to be the end all be all for self-motivation. Therefore, review your likes and dislikes. Understand what brings you joy so that you can stay motivated on this path you are pursuing.

Also, pinpoint boundaries you need to set with those around you to refrain from being triggered when experiencing repeat dislikes. Limit interactions with those people who bring out those feelings. You have the ability to take 100% control of your life by sticking to the discipline of putting your wellbeing first.

MOTIVATION IS KEY FOR THE HARD DAYS

"If you ever need to find motivation to accomplish something, try telling a few people what you are planning to do."

—**Aaron P. Taylor,** Author of *Be Thankful*

The reason self-motivation is so important to lock in continued success and wellbeing is that there are going to be days when you don't feel like making progress. You'll feel burned out when you focus on the same task each day. Or you might think that you have made no progress in a while, so what is the point? You'll need to determine the techniques that help you stay self-motivated so you can always remember what the point is. To be that change and to be of service to others.

We are always going through ups and downs throughout life, but it's essential to keep going. Keep creating a fulfilling life. Our **WHY** drives us. This **WHY** is the Life Purpose Statement you have created in Chapter 3. Why are you striving for this goal? Because you want to become the best version of yourself. Why are you developing an attitude of gratitude each day? Because you want to feel the benefits of being more positive and optimistic.

No matter what your why is, let it drive you each day to take action. Everyone is going to have a different 'why', and sometimes your 'why' is going to change for each new goal you put into place. But as long as you have your 'why', you'll have the motivation to keep pushing as hard as you can each day to obtain the biggest dreams you can think of.

Have your why written somewhere to keep driving your self-motivation. If you can remember that or read it every single morning, or before you go to bed, then you'll be able to bring it into your mind at a moment's notice. Never forget *why* you are striving hard each day. *Why* you are trying to improve yourself. *Why* you are trying to heal. *Why* you overcome the challenges in your life. Keep your 'why' fresh in your mind to drive you forward every day.

By doing so, you will trigger your RAS to bring in more resources, courses, people, and help to take you to where you want to be. You'll be surprised how many new opportunities appear when you keep in mind your why statement (life purpose statement). You are purpose-driven to achieve unique goals that reflect your passions in life. Never give up and never give in to the temptation of giving up. You are worth more than all your failures because of the colossal success that is waiting for you on the other side of all your hard work.

SELF-MOTIVATION IS ESSENTIAL

"Good things come to those who believe, better things come to those who are patient and the best things come to those who don't give up."

—**Ralph Smart,** British psychologist and author

The only sure way to achieve your goals and obtain everything that you set your mind to is by creating the ability to self-motivate. You won't have people in your life like your parents or teachers to provide external motivators. You'll need to build up your own inner strength that you can rely on when you need it most.

What this looks like is having such a deep sense of confidence in yourself that there is nothing that can take that feeling away from you. No future experience or what someone might say about your dream will put a dent in your confidence in yourself, your skills, and the path you're currently on. It is like your armor that protects you from outside influences.

If you have the desire . . .
If you have the drive . . .
If you have the focus . . .
If you have the grit . . .

Nothing and no one can stand in between you and what you're fighting for. You're only going in one direction—up and up.

When you have this belief in yourself, you'll be completely unstoppable.

DRIVE YOUR SELF-MOTIVATION

"It does not matter how slowly you go as long as you do not stop."

—**Confucius,** Chinese philosopher, poet, and politician

In order to drive your motivation every day, you're going to have to get clear on a handful of details surrounding your goals. You need to know *what* it is that you want. Why is it that you want to improve an aspect of your life? Think of the reason that you want to succeed and use that to fuel your fire. Even when things are seeming to become tough, remember your driving force to create change in your life and the life of others.

Another layer to driving your motivation is tapping into the emotions attached to both your successes and failures. When you've experienced a setback in the past, have you ever told yourself that you're not good enough? That emotional response to the roadblock causes your motivation to plummet. You can often be your biggest cheerleader, but you can also be a harsh judge as well.

When the time comes to self-motivate, focus on the positive state you want to be in. How does it make your body feel? How does it affect your energy levels? What messages are you telling yourself? How is your body language? Do this self-assessment to help you move towards a positive state if you realize that you're holding yourself back with doubt. By getting back into your groove and aligning yourself with positive thoughts and feelings, it will become easier to be self-motivated.

The team behind the online website Positive Psychology describes psychologist Scott Geller at the forefront of research on self-motivation, and he explains that there are three questions you can use to determine whether you (or someone in your life) are self-motivated:

1. Can you do it?
2. Will it work?
3. Is it worth it?

If you answered "yes" to each question, you are likely self-motivated.

If you believe you can do it, you have **self-efficacy**. If you believe it will work, you have response efficacy—belief that the action you are taking will lead to the outcome you want. And if you believe it is worth it, you have weighed the cost against the consequences and decided the consequences outweigh the cost (Geller, 2016).

Speaking of consequences, Geller considers "consequences" to be one of four vital "C" words that underpin self-motivation:

1. Consequences: To be self-motivated, you sincerely have to want the consequences associated with the actions you take, rather than simply avoiding negative consequences.

2. Competence: If you answer all three of the questions above with a "yes," you will feel competent in your ability to get things done.

3. Choice: Having a sense of autonomy over your actions encourages self-motivation.

4. Community: Having social support and connections with others is critical for feeling motivated and believing in yourself and your power to achieve (Geller, 2016).

Much of Geller's work on self-motivation is grounded in the research of psychologist and self-efficacy researcher Albert Bandura. In 1981, Bandura set the stage for Geller's current conceptualization of self-motivation with this description:

> *"Self-motivation . . . requires personal standards against which to evaluate ongoing performance. By making self-satisfaction conditional on a certain level of performance, individuals create self-inducements to persist in their efforts until their performances match internal standards. Both the anticipated satisfactions for matching attainments and the dissatisfactions with insufficient ones provide incentives for self-directed actions."* (Bandura & Schunk, 1981).

From this quote, you can see where Geller's three questions come from. Believing that you can do it, that it will work, and that it is worth it will drive you to match the internal standards you set for yourself.

WAYS TO SELF-MOTIVATE

While not every example is going to be the key that unlocks your motivational drive, these ideas will help you build an arsenal of tools to kick your goals into high gear. Try them out to see which ones click well with you.

- **Optimism–**
  Beware of the ANTs in the brain. These are automatic negative thoughts. Let them come and go through the mind, but never focus on them. Instead, stay focused on the positive. You got this!
- **Practice time management–**
  Set time aside each day to work towards your goals. This will not only give you something to look forward to each day, but will help you stop procrastinating.
- **Create a detailed action plan–**
  Nothing quite compares to seeing your goal and vision in black and white. Write what you want to obtain, along with your purpose statement. Then, create a list of bullet points that contain action steps. When you have a simple plan, it's easier to stick to compared to keeping the details locked away in your mind. Create a vision board with all the details of your plan that you can look at each day.
- **External success–**
  Sometimes when you feel stuck, you can rely on the success of others to give you that push to keep going. Whether this is an inspirational quote or learning the story behind the biggest leaders today, reflect on the success of those you admire to help you take the next step.
- **Music–**
  Every person deserves a theme song. What is yours? Having the right music playing can help us get into

the mood of plotting out action steps and putting them into motion. Create a playlist of your favorite songs to give you the extra pep in your step.

Binaural beats, two differing frequencies in each ear, at lower beta frequencies have been linked to improving memory and concentration.

- **Get outside–**
  Spending time in nature is proven to revitalize your soul and help you feel rejuvenated. It allows you to take a pause in your day and simply enjoy being still. Once you're able to recoup your energy, you can get back to working hard. When it's hard to take care of yourself, let nature take care of you.
- **Move–**
  Often we spend hours in front of the computer gathering resources, researching courses or people to connect with, and organizing major parts of the day. You need to get out and move. Whether this is a walk around the park or an hour at the gym, movement is key to progression and overall physical wellbeing.
- **Focus on one task at a time–**
  It won't help t feel pulled in every direction when you are trying to complete more than one goal at a time. Therefore, as you make your list of action steps for your plan, remember to take one task at a time.
- **Practice makes perfect–**
  Practice talking to yourself in front of the mirror. Remind yourself of all the progress you've made and what your next steps are. Remember, "If not me, then who?"

'If not me, then who?'

TRIANGLE OF POWER

Within an hour of waking up each day, I set myself up to take on the day. I create what I call the **triangle of power** within the first hour of getting out of bed. I spend time making food, working out, and cleaning my space. I stick to three things that I know are going to be good for my wellbeing, but also for my success. Having a clean space to work in helps me stay focused so I'm not distracted by any messes.

The three things you dedicate your time to in the morning may be different. You might enjoy meditating or reading before you get on with the rest of the day. Take the time to decide what your triangle of power is going to be first thing in the morning. This will boost your motivation and help you tackle the events of the day.

"We are what we repeatedly do. Excellence, then, is not an act, but a habit."

—**Aristotle,** Greek philosopher and polymath

Activity 9:
Techniques For Self-Motivation

It's time to make a list of all the techniques you're going to use to stay self-motivated. You can use the examples from this strategy or create your own.

For Example: Create my triangle of power every night for the next day. Put your goal on the calendar. Plan for imperfection. Watch a short motivational video on YouTube. Read a self-help book for 20 minutes. Exercise for 20 minutes.

#	Technique

"For me, becoming isn't about arriving somewhere or achieving a certain aim. I see it instead as forward motion, a means of evolving, a way to reach continuously toward a better self. The journey doesn't end."

—**Michelle Obama,** First Lady of the United States 2009–2017

Strategy 10. Take Action

"Happiness is not something ready-made. It comes from your own actions."

—**Dalai Lama XIV,** Spiritual leader and former Head of State of Tibet

In the book based on the research of 1000 entrepreneurs, *The Power of Focus* by Jack Canfield, Mark Victor Hansen, and Les Hewitt detail the findings of what made each entrepreneur successful. The key to this research is one of the most motivational things I've ever read. Every successful entrepreneur took responsibility, had unusual clarity and discipline, and was action-oriented.

These three attributes were represented in each successful entrepreneur, and every single one of them had to learn these life lessons in order to reach their success. That is because winners take action. It's one thing to talk about your dream. It's another to take action every single day, knowing that you can really do anything you set your mind to.

Have you ever been around a person who likes to talk a *lot* about what they are going to achieve? They have big plans for the future that seem awe-inspiring. But what happens when you run into them in a few weeks or months? They seem to still be talking about big plans without ever showing proof of taking action or making progress.

Actions will always speak louder than words. You don't need

to tell the world what you're going to achieve. You need to show others what you're capable of by committing to your goals and putting in the hard work each day. By knowing your passions, your why statement, and your purpose in life, you'll be guided to create measurable goals that are achievable.

Before you know it, people are going to see your accomplishments. You'll be able to lead by example, which leads to you teaching others about your process of success. Anyone can do it. It starts by taking action.

"I am experienced enough to do this. I am knowledgeable enough to do this. I am prepared enough to do this. I am mature enough to do this. I am brave enough to do this."

—**Alexandria Ocasio-Cortez**, American politician and activist

When you are working hard to achieve your goals and discover your passions, there will be times when you take the wrong action. You find yourself in a setback or facing an obstacle that wasn't on your path before. Now you are forced to stop and think about your next action step.

Whether your action steps are for your benefit or a mistake, take 100% responsibility for them. Be ready to fail because that is simply a part of success. Don't ignore failure or try to sweep it under the rug. Own that failure, be willing to admit that you've failed, and use that to propel you forward. Now you know what not to do in the future. You've discovered the key to success. Try and try again until you find the right answer. Never give up.

UNUSUAL CLARITY AND DISCIPLINE

When you're with your friends and they ask you what you want to eat during the night out, what is your answer? Oftentimes, we push the decision back on them, wanting to be considerate. "Oh,

I'll eat anything," might be your response. But in all honesty, what do you really want to eat? Do you want a burger with fries or pasta with pesto?

If we don't have clarity, the chances are higher that we won't even attempt to take action. We're not trained to sit down with ourselves and experience mindful moments where we can reflect on what we truly want to do. There is so much power in just sitting with yourself to understand what you want out of life and how you're going to accomplish that.

Having unusual clarity and discipline means having clear communication with yourself. You'll have to get into the habit of deciding, of being able to answer what you want to eat with detail and clarity. Your goals and actions need to have that same sense of clarity. Be able to explain your goal to anyone who asks about it with the details of how you're going to accomplish that goal.

Take action for yourself and always be clear with yourself about what you're about to do next. It requires a deep commitment to your success and wellbeing by becoming disciplined. You'll learn how to put yourself first and stop spending all your effort and energy helping others pursue their dreams. Reserve your strength and commitment for your own progression. You can support others without exhausting yourself in the process. It's time to take action just for *you*.

With discipline and self-control, we actually accomplish more of the goals we truly care about. Self-discipline is the bridge between defined goals defined and goals accomplished.

Chapter Eight of Brent Fleeson's book—*Embrace the Suck: The Navy SEAL Way To An Extraordinary Life*—is titled 'Win More Through Discipline And Accountability.' People with a higher degree of self-control debate less whether to indulge in behaviors and activities that don't align with their values or goals. They are more decisive. They don't let impulses or feelings dictate their choices. The actions they take to achieve the desired outcome are the architects of their own beliefs. As a result, they aren't as easily distracted by temptation and tend to feel more satisfied with their lives.

REPETITION IS KEY

We don't always succeed when we are taking relentless action and not meeting our goals as soon as we had planned. This is the time to remember that repetition is absolutely key. You can rest, but don't quit. Take your time to recoup your strength before taking action again.

When you are in action mode, people will gravitate towards you. The people you need to meet and the resources you've been looking for will come your way. People will see that you're in action mode and will come to understand what you are trying to accomplish. The right people will always support you. But it starts with being in action mode and staying there. You accomplish this by repetition and using the principles in this book on a daily basis. Even resting is still taking action.

The Law of Attraction is all about action. Even the word 'attraction' has the word 'action' in it. The universe has a way of bringing you everything you need for success when you enter action mode, stick to repetition, and keep striving for greatness each day. This is what it means to be action-oriented.

"The difference between a stumbling block and a steppingstone is how high you raise your foot."

—**Benny Lewis,** Irish author and blogger

Activity 10:
Build Momentum

Review the Wheel of Wellbeing. As you consider these areas again, think of an action step you can immediately take right away to build momentum towards your goals. Be specific with the date and time in which you'll complete this action step.

TIP: Review your goals created in Chapter 5 to clearly define one action step in each of these areas you can commit to accomplishing within the next week.

Example: To research and confirm a therapist by Friday, July 19, 5 pm EDT.

1. Personal life ________________________
2. Professional life ________________________
3. Health ________________________
4. Spiritual ________________________
5. Financial ________________________
6. Giving back ________________________
7. Hobbies ________________________

Strategy 11.
Pay It Forward

"Try to be a rainbow in someone's cloud."

—**Maya Angelou,** American poet, memoirist, and Civil Rights activist

To lock in success and wellbeing, it's important to lift others along the way. To really become a subject expert on a topic, you have to be willing to share that knowledge and teach others the same things you had to learn in order to become successful. Whether this is someone in your network or a younger person who could use a mentor. Always be willing to pay it forward wanting nothing in return. The universe has a way of rewarding those who give freely.

The best way to deeply learn a topic is to teach others. When I started hosting mental health workshops, I had goals and dates for the entire year marked on my calendar. I didn't know where I was going to host those meetings yet, or even if those future dates would work out with upcoming holidays. I just knew that I had to take action in order to see those goals become accomplishments. Having those dates laid out for the year was important and a part of setting very specific goals.

I didn't know all the topics for those workshops by heart, or the material I was putting together. This is where taking action took place in my life as I became clear with my goal and made the decision to commit. I made it a daily commitment to increase my training on the topics and to learn the material I was going to be providing. I created that higher level of motivation by doing it repeatedly. I did it for those that I knew I would be affecting. It brought me so much joy to pay my knowledge forward and give hope and guidance to those who were eager to grow themselves.

To keep me focused, I drafted an agenda for what each day was going to look like as I studied material and committed it to memory. Every month I taught that workshop, and with each event, I was improving my skills at presenting the topics.

Now, after five years, I can teach anyone about mental health and mental illness with my eyes closed. I don't need to look at my presentation besides briefly looking at a few words to remember the material. I have it memorized verbatim and can start talking about it at any time.

You also have a deep knowledge of a handful of topics that you know so well that you can start a conversation about them at any time. Maybe you're great at creating websites or computer coding. Or you know how to manage social media platforms like a pro. Perhaps you've mastered understanding healthy nutrition so that meal planning is no longer an overwhelming task.

You have cultivated many great skill sets over the years. When the opportunity arises, take the time to teach them to someone else. It can happen in a formal setting, or just on the go. You never know when the opportunity will come about, so simply have an openness to sharing your knowledge with others.

LEGACY MINDSET

"If you want to lift yourself up, lift up someone else."

—**Booker T. Washington,** American educator, author, orator, adviser to several presidents of the United States

We are all born for the reason of serving others and carry humanity forward. It is our purpose that helps us understand *how* we want to give back to our communities. When we can find what we are truly passionate about, we turn that passion into our purpose. This is the legacy that we leave behind. We'll be remembered for the impact we made on society and not how much money we made along the way. We are meant to inspire others to keep going, just like others have inspired us.

We are creating an impact for many to come after us as we pave a way for others to succeed as well. We create a solution to a problem and devote our lives to solving that one problem. And only when that solution no longer fulfills you and brings you happiness, then you can pass that legacy on to another to continue building while you create your next legacy. It's this constant cycle of creating, building, and serving that creates the foundation for your legacy.

Think about it this way. Every photo and video that you've created and posted on social media is a part of the legacy that you are leaving behind. Anyone can jump onto the internet and search for your content as a way to connect with you and relive past memories. Already you are creating a legacy to help the next generation by posting photos of your success and videos filled with your tips and tricks to live a successful life each day. You never know when someone is going to come across your video and be inspired by it.

Know that everything you are creating in your life, all the goals you are crushing, and the purposeful life you have established will one day be passed down to someone else. You'll pass that torch to the next generation as you then move forward to the next glorious adventure. It's okay to pursue a new legacy and passion when you become burnt out. Everything you created will go to the next individual who shares the same passion as you did.

At the beginning of the COVD-19 pandemic, I had published a book co-authored with Jack Canfield and other leading experts, *Success Strategies*. I had written one of the chapters. I remember talking to my mother while I was holding this book and said, "I just need you to know that I have done everything in my power at my capacity, at this age to learn from my mistakes, to learn how to heal myself, to try to make money and make you proud, to be independent and self-reliant, to be a good person and mean well. I need you to know that if anything were to happen to me that I am happy and fulfilled."

I said all of this while holding this book, so I added, "Mom, I know you haven't read this book, but I would really, really like you to. Hold on to this book because this is one of my legacies."

Co-authoring a book together with Jack Canfield is a part of the legacy that I am leaving behind. Sometimes we might not think that our accomplishments are a part of a legacy, but everything from a video to a book is a legacy that you are leaving behind. That is how you create a **legacy mindset** by realizing everything you do is a part of your legacy. It's going to help the next generation to come so they can solve more problems.

Glenn Llopis, in his article for Forbes titled '5 Ways A Legacy-Driven Mindset Will Define Your Leaders', stated, "It surprises me how many leaders don't spend enough time thinking about their legacy—what they will leave behind for the organization and the people they serve. Webster's dictionary defines legacy as, "anything handed down from the past, as from an ancestor or predecessor." Legacy is not bound by age or time served. Legacy represents your body of work at each stage of your career as you establish the foundational building blocks and accumulate the required wisdom to contribute to growth, innovation, and opportunity both in and outside of the workplace. Your legacy grows with each new experience, with each previously untested idea and bold ideal that you are courageous enough to deploy, and each time you inspire others to see something through to fruition."

GIVING BACK BY SUPPORTING OTHERS

"I slept and dreamt that life was joy. I woke up and saw that life was service. I acted and behold, service was joy."

—**Rabindranath Tagore,** Bengali Polymath, poet, writer, playwright, composer, and philosopher

I am always inspired every time I assist in one of Jack Canfield's training sessions. I get to meet the most amazing people who, even after retirement, are still chasing their passions and creating their next legacy. Whether it's at one of these trainings or supporting Jack on the backend, I'm constantly being introduced to people who never stop striving for their next goal while supporting others along the way.

Jack Canfield's long-term volunteer has been working with him for 25 years. Just recently, she published her first book. Immediately I wanted to support her and asked in what ways I could help. She's now organizing her own training sessions based on the principles of her book. You go, woman! It goes to show that it doesn't matter what age you are at. You continue to achieve greatness while supporting those around you at the same time.

There never comes a point where you'll feel content. You'll always be growing and reaching for that next level. When you're in the mindset of giving back, the universe is going to reward you. It helps you to create a discipline for helping others when you know the possibility of what you'll get back in return. It might not come right away, but eventually, it does come.

"If you knew what I know about the power of giving, you would not let a single meal pass without sharing it in some way."

—**Buddha,** Religious leader and teacher

Activity 11:
A Habit of Giving Back

When you give freely, you're allowing the universe to pay you back for all of your kindness, support, and encouragement to others. Use this time to reflect on the different ways in which you could give back.

Example: Donating food, clothes you haven't used in 6 months, stationary, leading free seminars, volunteering at a charity, hosting charity events, spending time with children at orphanages.

- ______________________________
- ______________________________
- ______________________________
- ______________________________
- ______________________________
- ______________________________
- ______________________________
- ______________________________
- ______________________________
- ______________________________
- ______________________________
- ______________________________
- ______________________________
- ______________________________
- ______________________________
- ______________________________
- ______________________________
- ______________________________

"We make a living by what we get, but we make a life by what we give."

—**Winston Churchill,** Former Prime Minister of the United Kingdom

Strategy 12. Unlock The Power of Self-Compassion

"At the end of the day, whether or not those people are comfortable with how you're living your life doesn't matter. What matters is whether you're comfortable with it."

—**Dr. Phil,** American TV personality and author

To lock in fulfillment in pursuing ongoing achievement, be aware that not everyone will extend the same level of kindness, grace, compassion, generosity, or love as you do. When unkind events occur, you need to show yourself kindness. No one can give you more compassion than what you can give yourself. In the most tough challenges of your life, you'll need to be prepared to show yourself grace.

At the same time my twin brother had passed away, I was also dealing with an expiring work permit for Canada. The company I was working for even hired a lawyer to renew my work permit, but it was rejected time and time again. I knew it was a sign that I needed to leave, rest and reset for a period. So, I wrapped everything up in Canada, renovated the condo, and by Jan 1, 2017, I left Canada for a month and a half.

With my parents, we went to the Ganges in India to release Tushar's cremains. It was a hard moment for me because both my parents broke down on my shoulders. I'm this tiny woman having to hold up both of my parents while they were able to release their emotions.

At that moment, I kept it together for my parents. That was the choice that I made to support them, even though I was falling apart on the inside. Afterward, we got back in the car to find something to eat. We ended up finding a small Dhaba, which is a roadside restaurant. The food was ready on the table. But I was still not feeling okay. While my parents had released their emotions, I chose not to.

While we were sitting, I could feel my frustrations growing. I ended up pulling out a book from my bag and told them to give me ten minutes. As I read, I noticed my nerves calmed down. The self-help book inspired me to believe that I am the creator of my present and future. I intentionally refocused my mind on what I could be grateful for, and I ended up shaping the rest of the trip to be one that was positive. I was motivated to submit all my documents for my Canadian permanent resident application and for my Canadian visitor's visa. I still had a ton of estate paperwork to wrap up for my late brother.

After this trip, I flew into San Francisco for a month to wait on my visitor's permit for Canada. I needed to get back so I could finish up so many things that I had put on hold. While I waited for my passport to show up, I reflected on everything I had experienced and had decided to start a mental health not-for-profit to help people maintain good mental health. When I made it back to Canada, the challenges didn't stop there.

"If you make your internal life a priority, then everything else you need on the outside will be given to you and it will be extremely clear what the next step is."

—**Gabrielle Bernstein,** New York Times best-selling author, motivational speaker, and podcast host

I stayed at different friends' places for a year because I couldn't get a rental. I didn't have any paystubs because I was self-employed and holding mental health workshops for my not-for-profit. Though I owned a property that I had leased out, I was no longer willing to stay there. My twin brother had passed away in that apartment.

I ended up leaving the country again when childhood friends of mine invited me on vacation in Thailand. It was such a magical experience because as soon as I arrived, I handed over my passport and just let them take care of me. They gave me the biggest room in the rental property. It was the first time I'd had my own space in a year. This space gave me the mental capacity to think differently. I showed myself grace. I decided to work with a different realtor who was able to have a rental property ready for me when I returned to Canada.

Creating space for healing is so important. Doing so for yourself and others helps you unlock the power of compassion. It's one of the greatest powers to master. This power is the ability to show understanding towards other people's situations. Help others create that space as well. Even if you meet someone in a food court, you can give them that space. Listening to them is creating that safe space.

We all know what we need to do, but still, we don't. We feel stuck or feel like there is something holding us back. But when you can create that space for yourself and show yourself compassion, you will know the right actions to take to move forward.

"The space we are in really contributes to our health and well-being," says Amy Wing, Occupational Therapist, Essentia Health. "The more comforting and soothing a space is, the easier it is for people to focus on their healing."

Based on this philosophy, the Miller-Dwan Foundation established a fund to help support the construction of a healing space in the Essentia Health hospital's adult inpatient psychiatric unit. "Providing a healing environment is integral to the overall care we provide," says Lainie Janke, Clinical Supervisor of Essentia Health Inpatient Behavioral Health. "Healing, by definition, means to make whole. All parts, including the environment, work together to create optimal healing for our patients."

Creating one in your own home can be a matter of simply rearranging your surroundings or including more natural elements. Here are five steps to help guide you in arranging your surroundings to foster good health.

1. Define the space by identifying what makes you feel comfortable and relaxed.
2. Declutter your healing space of objects that don't make you feel happy.
3. Invite nature by using natural light, incorporating landscape paintings or houseplants.
4. Use sounds that soothe, since sound is an important element in a healing space.
5. Set the mood with lighting, like exposing sunlight or using lights that mimic daylight.

TREAT YOUR INNER CHILD WITH LOVE AND CARE

Show yourself compassion by taking care of the inner child you're always carrying around. That playfulness you had as a child tends to die as you grow up. But in order to lock in ongoing success and wellbeing, keep that inner child alive through difficult and troubling situations. Dancing, painting, playing, and coloring help to bring back that inner child. You can run in a fun way or play sports with friends or even strangers.

My dad has come a long way. Today, he knows the importance of caring for his inner child. I can see that inner boy coming out when he's around me. Now he's so joyful and even asked if we could make a TikTok together the last time he visited. I was so surprised! We would bike together and do many things we never used to do. When he returned to Nigeria, he bought bikes for some of his friends. He wanted others to experience that feeling of bringing joy to their inner child.

When you lead by example, you'll be able to inspire everyone that sees that happiness in you. They'll want to know what makes you so happy and you'll have the opportunity to teach what you've learned brings happiness to your life. As you progress forward, never forget that you have an inner child that needs plenty of love and care as well.

SET BOUNDARIES AND SAY NO

I saw a big change in my father's life when he and my mother came to visit me in Canada after the passing of my twin brother. I showed them my condo and immediately my father complained about the little things—my velvet couch or the curtains over the window. I cut into his ranting to point out the fact that he had complained about my living space within ten minutes of stepping into the door. I said it in a joking way, but it seemed to get the message across.

I began setting boundaries with my dad, which resulted in an amazing transformation in him. Something changed. We were spending time together doing activities that we both loved to do. He was like a boy all over again.

I've never cut anyone out of my life. Even when someone is trying to convince me to do it because they believe it will be for my own wellbeing, I won't do it. Instead, I set boundaries. I choose not to spend a lot of time with them. It's okay to say 'no' to people and projects that don't add any value to the wheel of wellbeing.

The first step in learning to set boundaries is to uncover what your personal limits and guidelines are. In her TEDx talk, Sarri Gilman, MA, MFT, a psychotherapist and author of *Transform*

Your Boundaries, explains that we can think of our boundaries through the metaphor of an inner compass with two words written on it: *Yes* and *No*.

We all have an inner sense of wisdom, which intuitively tells us when something is a yes or a no. The problem arises when we ignore or argue with that inner voice. If you are not used to tuning into your intuition, it is important to practice paying attention to how you are feeling in the moment. Using tools such as meditation and mindfulness is one way to practice paying attention to your thoughts and feelings in the moment.

"Boundary setting will unleash emotions," Gilman says. "When you listen to your own yes and no," other people may get angry or disappointed. The reality is that whenever you set boundaries with people, they may not have a pleasant reaction. However, you still can work to firmly maintain the boundaries that you have set.

Setting boundaries with people can actually help to improve your relationships in the long run. If you do not respect your personal boundaries (perhaps in fear of someone else's reaction), it is likely to lead to bitterness and resentment over time. The people you want to surround yourself with are those who will respect your boundaries, even if they initially feel upset or disappointed.

Setting boundaries can be difficult but is such an important part of having healthy relationships and establishing an overall sense of wellbeing. It's helpful to remember that when you say "no" to things, it frees up your time to focus on the pursuits that truly energize and excite you. Having good boundaries also enables you to experience less stress and to follow your life's passion and purpose.

"Boundaries define us. They define what is me and what is not me. A boundary shows me where I end and someone else begins, leading me to a sense of ownership. Knowing what I am to own and take responsibility for gives me freedom."

—**Henry Cloud,** American self-help author

Activity 12:
Write Yourself A Compassionate Letter

Write yourself a letter from the stance of being a senior for example eighty years old. What would you want your younger self to know?

The next letter is going to be from a younger version of yourself. What do you want to tell your future self who just turned eighty or more?

PART FOUR

Advanced Tactics For Exceptional Results

Strategy 13. Take Care of Your Wealth

"As you can see, wealth isn't necessarily about money; it is more the wealth that you have within your own soul and what comes through your mouth and heart."

—**Catherine Pulsifer,** Author

I was one of the youngest to be accepted into Jack Canfield's program. While I was going through the training, I was surrounded by successful entrepreneurs who were retired or getting ready to retire. I know how fortunate I was to be surrounded by so many people who had achieved their dreams and were still reaching new heights.

Through this community, I learned that building anything onward and upward happens when you take care of your wealth. While this word automatically triggers thoughts about money, what I am referring to is true wealth.

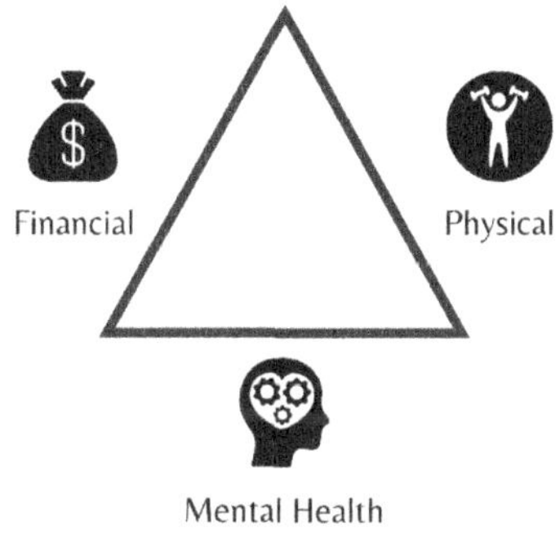

The **Triangle of Wealth** comprises physical, financial, and mental health. The ultimate achievement of being wealthy is the combination of all three. It's more than just having money. Being healthy in all three areas is what it's about. This strategy is dedicated to teaching you how to strengthen all three areas so they become an equal triangle. Society focuses so much on just money that most people then put their physical and mental health off to the side to take care of later. But the only way to be wealthy and successful in life is to balance all three.

When I was doing a Grant Cardone training, I remember being unable to put down any details about my relationships and family while filling out the activity for the day. After everything I'd experienced in my life and the challenges I was still facing, it was hard to put into words my current relationship with my family.

It wasn't until I sought professional help after returning from my trip to India that I was empowered to better take care of my needs. By investing in myself consistently, I could then build strong connections with friends and my family. It allowed me to write all the details about them during the activities in the program.

Build your wealth by focusing on improving your physical, financial, and mental health. Know that challenging moments will always show up and there will always be healing to do. But you are capable of making the right choices to heal, to navigate, to change the narrative in order to continue to build your wealth.

"We must let go of the life we have planned, so as to accept the one that is waiting for us."

—**Joseph Campbell,** American writer

Sometimes it's hard to see my friends with their siblings, progressing their businesses together. It makes me miss my brothers as we once dreamed of running successful businesses together.

When these feelings occur from everything I feel I'm missing out on, I have to realize that I can still build that wealth. The old programming is a matter of habit. Today I am grateful for real friends who are like family. I have people I collaborate with and partner with that I am very loyal to. I know now that relationships make you wealthier when you form those deep connections.

What happened, happened. What do I have from it? On a deeper level, I have great opportunities to connect with people. I take the first steps towards creating these relationships. I take care of my triangle of wealth by focusing on all three instead of just one aspect.

IMPROVE YOUR PHYSICAL HEALTH

Being aware of how active you are every day and what you put into your body are both important to keep your body healthy. By creating positive physical habits, you'll in turn have more energy and decrease your stress.

1. **Get Active–**
   Moving more each day has major health benefits. It is said that adults need two and a half hours of moderate physical activity each week. You'll achieve this too when you set specific goals for your physical health. This can be taking the stairs instead of the elevator when you get to work or parking your car at the far end of the parking lot to get in those extra steps. Set time aside every day to be active.
2. **Maintain Your Muscles–**
   It's important to build muscle so you can keep enjoying the activities that you love. It is recommended to do strength training two or more days a week. Start slowly, pay attention to your body, and use small weights in the beginning. It's important to move

slowly and steadily until you can gain more experience.

3. **Find A Healthy Weight–**
   Take charge of your weight. It starts by eating healthy by including plenty of colorful vegetables in your diet. When you increase how active you are each day, you'll see how every little bit counts. It's important to remain realistic and aim for slow weight loss.
4. **Mind Your Metabolism–**
   As you get older, your metabolism is going to change. This requires you to exercise more and to adjust your diet. To combat these changes, commit to a healthy diet, which includes drinking plenty of water. Make sure you are getting plenty of sleep. Consider limiting your alcohol use and avoiding tobacco products altogether.
5. **Build Healthy Habits–**
   Though we all know that healthy habits make us feel better, it's difficult to start a new habit. Plan to create habits by understanding your triggers and setting realistic goals. It helps to track your progress to ensure you're on the right path and being patient with yourself. Sometimes it takes a year to really see the change. Imagine your future self after sticking to your new healthy habits to motivate you to keep pushing hard each day.

Developing the right habits (and getting rid of the wrong ones) is key to any effective health plan. While the strategies in this book can apply to business, child-rearing, or productivity, they'll also help you form the foundation for better health.

Whether you want to lose weight, manage anxiety, or reduce stress, *The Power of Habit* by Charles Duhigg will help you develop the right habits so you can reach your goals and keep making progress toward a better you.

6. **Eat A Healthy Diet–**
   When you build your healthy diet, don't focus so much on the foods you can't eat but on the foods that you can. There are many healthy options that all you have to do is plan to enjoy good food instead of focusing on what you must avoid. Start trying a variety of new foods to see what you like the most so you can create your new go-tos when you have a busy day.

   In *How Not to Die*, Dr. Michael Greger examines the top fifteen natural causes of premature death and explains how simple diet and lifestyle changes can help you avoid them without prescriptions or surgeries.

   Besides listing the best foods we should consume in order to avoid the leading causes of death, *How Not to Die* also includes a checklist of the twelve foods that should be part of our daily diets. Backed by strong scientific evidence, Dr. Greger's advice has the potential to save lives and improve the health of millions.

IMPROVE YOUR FINANCIAL HEALTH

Having financial health is all about understanding the money that you are making and ensuring that each dollar is being spent to support your purpose statement. For many in society, money comes and goes like the wind. But to have financial health, you need to know your money just as well as your best friend.

1. **Track Your Expenses–**
   Ever get to the end of the month and wonder where

all of your money has gone? Don't be left in the dark anymore by tracking your expenses. Whether you like to use an Excel file to write what you spent money on each month, or you keep a notebook to categorize how you spend your money, you need to see where your money is going each month in order to make changes.

2. **Identify Your Bad Money Spending Habits–**
   By tracking your expenses, especially when you do it for the first time, you'll see all of your bad money spending habits. Identify where you're spending the most of your money each month, whether it's on coffee or fast food, and decide if this is for your own good or not. Know what your bad money spending habits are and their triggers to control that spending in the future.

3. **Know Your Net Worth–**
   Most people have no clue what that number is. It's more than understanding what you make each month or year. It is the total value of all financial or non-financial assets owned by you, minus the value of any outstanding liabilities you owe. You must know your net worth in order to set a realistic goal that inspires you to stay motivated.

4. **Budget–**
   The most successful entrepreneurs in the world who make millions a year still have a budget. They understand the amount that they make each year, and they have a job for every dollar. Therefore, take the time to set a budget for your money. The only way to reach financial goals is by putting your money to work. Understand all of your income, expenses, what can be cut, and where your money can grow.

5. **Pay Yourself First–**

You need to take care of both your physical and mental health. Therefore, how is your financial health going to ensure that? Make sure you pay yourself first before you spend on others.

6. **Invest–**
   To have true financial freedom, you must save to invest as soon as possible. Whether this is a Roth IRA, real estate, stocks, mutual funds, cryptocurrency or adding more to your retirement plan from the company you work for, you need to invest in your future. Utilize the free financial services from your bank to get started. Create those relationships with financial advisors you can rely on to help you build financial freedom.

"When it comes to luck, you make your own."

—**Bruce Springsteen,** American singer-songwriter

IMPROVE YOUR MENTAL HEALTH

My passion for mental health advocacy and education could fill the pages of its own complete book. I can't stress enough the importance of strengthening your mental health. Not only to overcome the challenges of the future but to heal from the traumas of the past. When you have this mental strength, you can accomplish anything.

1. **Set A Routine For Rest–**
   Getting up in the morning and going to bed at similar times every day has huge benefits for strengthening your mental health. Rest and proper sleep are essential to your wellbeing. Ensuring to make this a routine of similar times each night and morning will help you have a stronger mindset.

2. **Personal Hygiene–**
   When you dress your best, you feel good. It feels good to take a long shower, use your favorite products, and get ready for the day by styling your hair or wearing makeup that makes you feel special. All of these good feelings come from keeping up with personal hygiene. When you take care of yourself, you'll be able to build those positive feelings each morning to support your mental health throughout the day. Even washing your hands in the middle of the day, taking your time, and treating yourself will help during stressful situations.
3. **A Routine of Eating Healthy–**
   We all know that eating healthy helps us feel better about ourselves. After you're done eating, you feel that sense of satisfaction. That is why it's important to have a routine of healthy eating. Not just a few times a week or once a week, but every day. Taking care of your body will reflect on your mental health. Knowing you're making the right decisions helps you strengthen your mind that you can achieve anything.
4. **Exercise Regularly–**
   When you're active, your brain releases dopamine. Hence the reason for the 'athlete's high' and why exercise can be addicting. You feel great after a good workout session. When you are experiencing depression, go for a walk. Moving and staying active helps regulate positive hormones in the body.
5. **Time For Work. Time For Rest–**
   Allocating time for both work and rest to create a balance is very important to your mental health. Sometimes it's compelling to just work, work, work all day, every day. But you need physical and mental rest to sustain achievement. Set time aside each day

to be in a state of rest. Whether that is reading a book or listening to your favorite music while you dance around your apartment, rest your mind from all the work you do each day.

6. **Make Time For You–**
   A few times in this book you've had space to write out the things that you enjoy doing. But it's equally important to schedule time in your day to do those things. Make time for doing the small and big things that you enjoy to help balance the time you might spend stressing at work.

"Dreams don't have to just be dreams. You can make it a reality; if you just keep pushing and keep trying, then eventually you'll reach your goal. And if that takes a few years, then that's great, but if it takes 10 or 20, then that's part of the process."

—**Naomi Osaka,** Japanese tennis player

Activity 13:
Your Triangle of Wealth

This is a self-awareness activity that will help you determine the current state of your Triangle of Wealth.

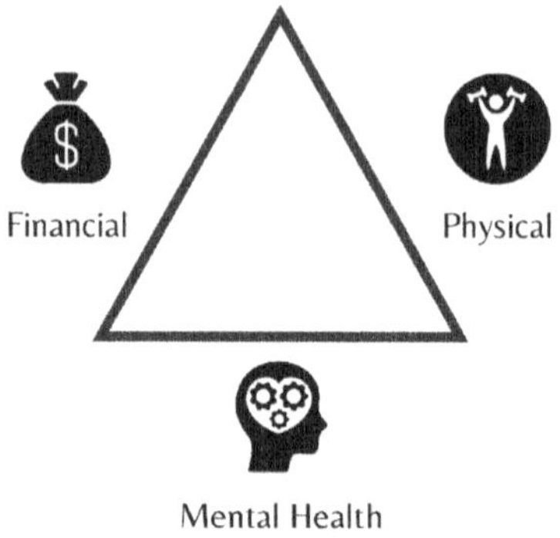

Which areas are you not happy with?

____

____

Which ones do you want to improve?

____

____

Which ones feel incomplete?

____

____

One action step I will immediately take is . . .

____

____

Strategy 14. Mindful Living

"You must find the place inside yourself where nothing is impossible."

—**Deepak Chopra,** Indian-American author and alternative medicine advocate

When we are told something that we don't particularly like, whether it comes from our boss, our parents, a sibling, or a partner, it triggers the **amygdala** in our brains. That's the part of our brains that handles our ability to fight or flight in extreme situations. It causes **adrenaline** to pump into our bodies so we can either fight off the attacker or run as fast as we can away from the situation.

The part of the brain that we want to initiate when we receive negative talk is the **prefrontal cortex**. The role it plays is to calm the amygdala, and we're able to activate this when we name our emotions and feelings. This allows us to put a pause to reacting to the amygdala, so we can control our responses.

The amygdala helped humankind back in the day when we were a race of hunters and gatherers because it protected us. It gave us the ability to survive in the harshest of environments when there was danger around us. The amygdala would light up when we needed to run, shouting, "Danger! Danger! Danger!" It can wake us up from a deep sleep to protect ourselves.

Today we still have the amygdala as part of our anatomy, but we are not living in environments where we need to fight against animals. Now we are going through different situations where the amygdala will fire when it senses that we are in some kind of danger. Including receiving negative talk from those in our close environment. Our prefrontal cortex controls our thoughts and actions, giving us a moment before we respond to the distress the amygdala has picked up.

"If my mind can conceive it, if my heart can believe it, then I can achieve it."

—**Muhammad Ali,** American professional boxer

The practice of mindful living is to become more aware of how we react to each event. We can all establish the practice of redirecting negative thoughts into a positive experience. Regardless of what someone might say to you, always remember that there is a part of the brain that controls all thoughts and feelings. You are in charge of that brain, and you determine your thoughts, emotions, and behaviors. By shifting to a positive mindset, you create more positive outcomes.

You have the power to choose a different response, even during the most difficult situations. Your emotional alarm system is still going to be triggered as adrenaline rushes through the body. You'll want to have an immediate response to all events, but you can choose what that response is instead of letting the event choose for you.

For a great introduction to mindfulness that is grounded in Buddhist teachings, Thích Nhất Hạnh's book *The Miracle of Mindfulness* explains mindfulness using everyday examples paired with pragmatic recommendations.

PUT ON THE BRAKES

Mindful living is largely in part to living with more awareness. It is very easy to ignore aspects of our lives when we are only focused on working or making money. Shifting your focus to be more aware of what is happening internally and how you react to all situations is mindfulness. This is how you become 100% in control of your life.

One of the biggest tools at your disposal is the ability to put the brakes on when your thoughts are racing and your emotional distress level is getting high. This allows you to think about your response instead of instinctively reacting. You're activating your prefrontal cortex instead of letting your amygdala run the show.

By practicing mindfulness, you become more attuned with how you react to situations and instead focus on the desired outcomes you'd like to cultivate. Just like noticing your breath during meditation, you're recognizing yourself more than you ever have in your life.

"There is nothing impossible to they who will try."

—**Alexander the Great,** Former King of Macedonia

When I was progressing through Jack Canfield's *Train The Trainer* course, each day started with 20 minutes of meditation. It was hard for me to get into the routine of sitting with myself and not doing anything. I've learned over the years that one way to respond to trauma is to always want to go, go, go. Spending this time being still was difficult for me as I practiced meditation for the first time.

For the first few days, I couldn't help but keep my eyes open and look around, a smile on my face as I peeked at these successful individuals around me. My inner child was having a lot of fun feeling silly in those few first moments.

After a few days of feeling silly, I knew I wanted to understand what my peers were experiencing after these 20 minutes of meditation. So, I forced myself to close my eyes, even if I had to keep smiling through the entire session. As I closed my eyes, I thought about all sorts of things as I went through the motions.

But when the time came for me to open my eyes, I realized I had tears running down my face.

The next day, I decided I was going to do it again and added to this practice that it was okay not to focus. I would not be hard on myself for not reaching a moment of peace and instead kept bringing my attention back to the moment. If I couldn't do that, I focused on my breath. When I opened my eyes again, I still had tears in my eyes.

By the end of the training, I felt something I had never felt before. It was a feeling of euphoria that was completely organic and natural. It was pure joy mixed with a sense of peace. I was still my passionate self, but I had the feeling of being centered that I was never taught before.

What this experience taught me about becoming more aware of myself is that you must do it all for yourself. Don't reject the healing or the source of joy. Instead, set your intention to live a life that is filled with joy. Being mindful is deciding not to live by the seat of your pants any longer. With intent, you're going to get something out of this life, and more importantly, this book.

TIPS FOR MINDFULNESS

1. **Set Your Intention–**
   When there is no intention, there is no *tension.* It is the tension and the feeling of being somewhere uncomfortable that is going to be your biggest teacher. Practice meditation (silent or guided) to become aware of yourself and create a habit of mindful living.

2. **Give Yourself Permission To Just Be–**
   Never feel guilty about standing still. You don't always need to be on the go. Just be yourself at this moment, knowing that life will still go on. Take the time for yourself.

3. **Choose Your Form of Expression–**
   Some like to sing, others like to paint. Some need a moment to cry, while others need to jump into the deep end of the swimming pool and scream underwater. Whatever you need to express yourself, do it. Choose a form and express yourself instead of suppressing your emotions.

4. **Eat With Awareness–**
   It is easy to get into the routine of eating the same things every day or grabbing food on the go. Bring awareness back to what you are putting into your body. If you realize that you're not eating good foods, decide to make the change for your continued wellbeing.

5. **Clear Your Environments–**
   Take check of the areas that you spend the most time in. Sometimes they need a good deep cleaning. This can reflect both your physical environment, but also your mental space as well. Take the time to clear the clutter, let your mind relax, and create space for those things you want to focus on.

6. **Start Your Day With Something Unique To You–**
   We are all different. My mentor teaches the hour of power method, which is 20 mins of meditating, 20 mins of reading and 20 mins of exercising. I love the idea of an hour of power. But for me, I juice, clean, and make breakfast to get my day started. Start your day with something unique to you to bring more awareness to your day.

7. **Ground Yourself Physically–**
   Grounding in the principle of being rooted in what you are trying to accomplish. Sometimes the events of life can throw you off balance. You're being pulled in so many directions and can't seem to find healing

for your state of distress. Being grounded allows you to stand tall and strong. Find the ability to be grounded in all that you do with mindful living to withstand the storms of life. Find that inner healing as you notice what parts of you need healing.

8. **Practice Deep Breathing–**
   When you sleep, you breathe with your belly. But during the day, most of the breathing happens with the diaphragm. Practice deep breathing to fill your lungs completely. You must focus your mind to do this, which causes your thoughts to be pulled away from being nervous and anxious. Now you just focus on deep breathing to become grounded and aware once more.

One great thing about mindfulness is that there is not just one way to practice it. You may find which one works best for you in these 75 exercises that Matthew Sockolov details in his book *Practicing Mindfulness: 75 Essential Meditations to Reduce Stress, Improve Mental Health, and Find Peace in the Everyday*. Full of brief 5-to-15-minute exercises, this book will help you build a sustainable mindfulness practice and tackle some of the common challenges, such as a wandering mind that beginners often experience.

"The bad news is time flies. The good news is you're the pilot."

—**Michael Altshuler,** Keynote speaker, peak performance, and sales gladiator

Activity 14:
Decoding Your Response

Understanding the science behind how your brain reacts when experiencing stress and distress is key to becoming more aware of how you react to difficult situations. During this activity, take the time to decode how you currently respond to negative events.

What does your amygdala tell you to do in a difficult situation? For example, does your heart race? Do you feel jumpy or on edge? What responses happen in the bad that have been triggered by your amygdala and adrenaline?

____

____

What does your prefrontal cortex tell your amygdala in order to put on the breaks? What thoughts and feelings start to swim through your mind once your brain has detected stress?

____

____

Below, write down your top five instincts and a time when you felt them. What is an immediate response that you normally have when a difficult situation arises?

Example: I yell or cry when my partner tells me to have it all together.

I feel like . . . when . . .

1. ____________________________________
2. ____________________________________
3. ____________________________________
4. ____________________________________
5. ____________________________________

Now, review those feelings and actions in order to write down what are the consequences (outcomes) of that response.

Example: Punishment, making someone angry, upsetting someone, or making someone cry.

1. ______________________________________
2. ______________________________________
3. ______________________________________
4. ______________________________________
5. ______________________________________

This activity helps you to become more mindful of yourself and the responses that you instinctively take when distress arises. Really think of a time when you had to respond that did not make you feel good. Remember those consequences. Use this information to become aware of your urges and how you can put a pause in that response phase to really think about the outcomes you'd like to experience in the future.

> *"When I was 5 years old, my mother always told me that happiness was the key to life. When I went to school, they asked me what I wanted to be when I grew up. I wrote down 'happy'. They told me I didn't understand the assignment, and I told them they didn't understand life."*
>
> —**John Lennon,** Singer-songwriter

Strategy 15. Use Optimism In Every Aspect Of Life

"If you're reading this . . .
Congratulations, you're alive.
If that's not something to smile about,
then I don't know what is."

—**Chad Sugg,** Author of *Monsters Under Your Head*

When we're not feeling well, it's easy for us to go back into our old habits. It's hard to create success in any area of life when negative emotions are taking hold of every thought and action. This is why it's important in REAL-TIME to focus on the good. Think about your responses to the event, how you are feeling, and what results you would rather have. Especially in the heat of the moment.

Therefore, mindfulness is important because it forces you to take that break and let the frontal cortex do its job. When you think about the end results, you can choose a different response. This is the genuine power that you possess right now, regardless of what life has thrown at you.

When I wasn't feeling good with what life had thrown at me, I was relentless in my pursuit of wellbeing. I wanted to work with a therapist to persevere, to take care of myself, to thrive. Initially, I worked with someone I didn't like. The connection wasn't there, and I didn't feel like I was benefiting from it. But I didn't reject the idea of working with a therapist. I went and found another therapist I could jive with.

When you don't have good wellbeing, you can't communicate with your teammates, your friends or your family effectively. It's important to communicate well and intentionally be in a place of wellbeing. Focus on the good and activities that bring you joy. Count 5-4-3-2-1 and make a conscious choice to change your thoughts and actions. It wasn't until the fourth therapist that things started to work for me. I'm so glad that I didn't quit. I didn't give up on the idea of improving my wellbeing. Instead, I focused on the good.

The Glass Half-Full by Suzanne Segerstrom takes scientific studies further and shows us that being an optimist can help you get ahead in life. Segerstrom is one of the top psychologists working on optimism and pessimism. The thing that she has found out through her research, and what she writes about in her book, is that optimism isn't just about thinking. A lot of self-help books assume that optimism and pessimism are all about the way we think. But Segerstrom makes the strong point that optimism is also about what you do.

What she found was that optimistic people were more likely to solve it and not to give up. She thinks that this persistence at a task is one of the key things that helps optimists to become more successful in life because they simply try harder and stick with things for longer. There is a can-do attitude which is absolutely the optimistic mindset that will translate into actions.

PRACTICE POSITIVE SELF-TALK

"Optimism is a strategy for making a better future. Because unless you believe that the future can be better, you are unlikely to step up and take responsibility for making it so."

—**Noam Chomsky,** American linguist, philosopher, cognitive scientist, and historical essayist

An amazing tool for those who use it, the Mirror Exercise created by Louise Hay to acknowledge yourself and help your mind become more optimistic instead of always focusing on the negative.

She explains that "Mirror work is the most effective method I've found for learning to love yourself and see the world as a safe and loving place. I have been teaching people how to do mirror work for as long as I have been teaching affirmations."

To practice this method, stand in front of a mirror and begin a conversation with yourself by saying your name out loud and acknowledging the things you did on the day that you didn't like. Then talk about the things you are good at. Validate your actions as you tell that person in the mirror your accomplishments and wins. Always end by saying, "I love you."

Take time away from social media to create space just for yourself. All too often, we work hard to create a certain type of persona for people to see on a screen. But Mirror Work is about spending time with just your authentic self. No one is going to be watching, and you will not be recording yourself or taking a picture. If you can commit to it, make it a goal to do this once a day for three weeks. You'll watch your self-esteem go way up.

SPEND TIME WITH POSITIVE PEOPLE

"If you don't like the road you're walking, start paving another one!"

—**Dolly Parton,** American singer-songwriter

Have you ever walked into a room during a seminar, conference, or training and felt the surge of energy because you know that you're amongst others who want to learn and have a positive mindset? It's like entering a stadium to watch your favorite sports team and have an instant connection with other fans who just want to have a good time. There is nothing quite like being around those that are always uplifting, motivational, and inspiring.

But you don't need to attend a seminar or conference to be around positive people. Think of those who are your friends or part of your family that you always feel good around. It could be a grandparent or a friend who has established a positive mindset. They are always happy, and that happiness is contagious. Spend time with these individuals to boost your own optimistic mindset.

If you can't be around others who are positive, then take the time to listen or watch motivational documentaries, movies, or TED Talks. This is a great exercise to do before going to bed and first thing in the morning. Swap scrolling through social media by watching a motivational video and reflecting on it. There are loads of positive speakers you can connect with digitally that will help you create the optimistic mindset that you can use each day.

USE AFFIRMATIONS TO REWIRE YOUR BRAIN

"If you have good thoughts they will shine out of your face like sunbeams and you will always look lovely."

—**Roald Dahl**, British novelist, short-story writer, poet, screenwriter, wartime fighter of Norwegian descent

At the beginning of this book, you created an affirmation for each goal. If you have been practicing reciting your affirmations daily, you must have already seen a difference in your motivation levels and how you feel. There is great power in reciting affirmations multiple times a day to bring you closer to the point of success you are currently reaching for.

At one seminar I had attended, I met a lady, Christie Miller, who shared a story of winning a Porsche Cayenne from a contest. She would write over 100 times daily that she had already won the contest and visualize how it felt to be sitting in it, driving it around, and how it made her feel. She once went to a local car dealership to test drive the car. She had a toy car on her desk to remind her daily. In 2018, she won a black Porsche Cayenne.

Now that was a car she attracted! Let's think of one thought you often have that is negative. Something you are aware of that you want to improve. Write that unique affirmation to rewire your mind to think positively. Write it down somewhere that you can see it every day until you are able to commit it to memory. Once you know your affirmation like the back of your hand, you can recite it throughout the day. On your way to work, during your lunch break, and when you are falling asleep at night.

Your affirmations become the mantras that help you keep your mind focused on achieving what you want—better health, better relationships, a promotion or anything materialist. During challenging moments, these mantras keep you focused. You are moving forward with an optimistic mindset. Let those positive feelings wash over you and clear out your mental space.

"Find out who you are and be that person. That's what your soul was put on this earth to be. Find that truth, live that truth, and everything else will come."

—**Ellen DeGeneres**, American comedian, television host, actress, writer and producer

Activity 15: Stop And Think

Think back to a negative event in your life.

How did you respond?

____

____

What emotions did you feel by choosing your conditioned response?

____

____

What emotions would you have rather experienced?

____

____

How could you have responded instead?

____

____

"Optimism is essential to achievement and it is also the foundation of courage and true progress."

—**Nicholas M. Butler**, Former President of Columbia University, philosopher, diplomat and educator

Strategy 16. Recharge Your Vision, Goals, and Affirmations

"In this game everyone needs a break to refuel, recharge, and jump back in full throttle."

—**Helen Edwards,** Author of *Nothing Sexier Than Freedom*

How many times have you started a new hobby, goal, activity, or career only to discover that it doesn't bring you joy? One of the most wonderful parts of life is that each day you can make the choice to start anew. Every day is filled with new possibilities, and there are many things that you can try out. There is a never-ending list of activities that you can discover. But just because you've committed time to one of these activities or one career doesn't mean you need to stick with it. If it doesn't bring you joy, it's time for something else.

Reevaluate your goals periodically to ensure that you are still finding joy in the process. We're all subject to change, and what might have once brought you happiness and excitement might one day feel boring and unfulfilling. You'll discover this when you take the time to evaluate your goals to ensure that you are still passionate about them.

This will also help you discover if you are still motivated towards these goals or if there is now some sort of obstacle in your way. When facing a wall, it's easy to decide not to climb over it when you don't have the right tools to make the climb. In this strategy, you'll discover the many ways in which you can recharge your vision, goals, and affirmations, as well as find the right solutions to the roadblocks you are facing with your goals.

There are two fundamental life principles my older brother taught me during his time on earth. He taught me and my twin how to have an attitude of gratitude, but also the power of review. This included how to stop and think about what you are trying to accomplish to ensure you are still on the right track or if you've veered off the path by even an inch.

When charting a course through the air or sea, being off your target by even a few centimeters can land you in another part of the world than where you were expecting. The same thing can happen when we are chasing our dreams and don't take the time to review our progress and where the present course is leading us.

Reevaluate your vision, goals, and affirmations to ensure they are still guiding you towards the success you are chasing. Update your affirmations to reflect the present course of action you are taking. And determine what's standing in your way that now needs to be addressed in order to move forward. You have the power to change every day if you want to. You are in full control now.

UNDERSTANDING THE ROADBLOCKS

"You are never too old to set another goal or to dream a new dream."

—**C. S. Lewis,** British writer

There is a great depth in understanding potential roadblocks on your pathway to success. It can be something small, like needing to set the time aside to work on your goals or gain a new skill set. Or it can be losing interest and not wanting to take action when there is already so much on your plate. You could also heal an incomplete part of your life, whether that is physical or mental health.

Kerri Adams, a psychotherapist based out of Toronto, Canada, once shared with me something interesting about a muscle of resilience we all possess. Every day we face some obstacle or the other. It could be something as simple as your partner not answering your call or your coworker not doing their job diligently or the food you ordered home didn't get delivered to your house. This muscle of resilience is absorbing these events as and when they occur. You process them mindfully and choose a response to move forward. But at some point, if too many troubling or difficult situations occur in our lives at the same time, that muscle gets overwhelmed, and it starts to bounce off. This looks like feelings of irritability, snappiness, anger, overwhelm, anxiety, isolation, or depression. This is why it is important to give yourself a break to rest, give yourself permission to observe, process, practice mindfulness in those moments, and reach out for help.

This can be a major roadblock on your path to success if you haven't released the negative emotions of past traumas. You can only work so hard before you'll feel burnt out or overwhelmed with everything on your plate. Observe these roadblocks, choose to heal, and then you'll finally be able to move forward.

One way to overcome a roadblock is to reach out to people for feedback who would be unbiased and mean well for you. For every problem, there is an expert who can help with the solution. You'll learn more about sharing and receiving feedback in Strategy 18, but for now, know that gaining that different perspective can often give you the review and guidance you need to sustain success and wellbeing.

ATTEND TRAINING SEMINARS

"Learning is not attained by chance, it must be sought for with ardor and attended to with diligence."

—**Abigail Adams,** Former First Lady of the United States

One of the greatest ways to recharge your vision and goals is to be surrounded by people who share the same passions as you. Attend training seminars in the area that you want to improve. The most successful people are the ones that are always investing in their growth. Train specifically in what you are doing and want to grow in. It helps to recharge and inspire you to take action all over again.

When you are finished with any sort of training seminar, it's important to take a break in order to incorporate all the new information or new inspiration into your life. So many people keep investing in different courses without taking the time to apply their learnings. They get burnt out with the knowledge and wonder why there are no results.

Instead, review your notes from the seminar. That's how my older brother would always get high scores on his tests. He would never cram before giving a test, but he would simply review his notes often. As you finish up a training session, review the notes you've taken before you take action.

SURROUND YOURSELF WITH HIGH VIBING PEOPLE

Have you ever heard of a mastermind group before? It's a popular term in the world of success, but very few take part in one. It's run very strategically where everyone in the group comes with their own set of skills. Imagine a small room filled with masters coming together to offer advice to one another in a professional setting. It's a meeting where you'll leave 100% inspired to take action.

In this day and age, mastermind groups happen in the digital space. It's easy to hop onto an online meeting to meet with all sorts of masters from around the world. You'll be given time to share what you are currently working on to receive advice and feedback. In turn, you will offer your knowledge and expertise. If you get the chance to participate in a mastermind group, do it!

Tony Robbins explains, "An ideal mastermind group brings

together businesspeople at different levels of success and with different strengths and weaknesses. This way, each member can lend their strengths to other members of the group and work on their weaknesses. Mastermind groups will help you question your limiting beliefs, face your fears and challenge you to do better every day."

If that is not something you'd be interested in, consider then having an accountability partner. This can still be a structured resource where you call your accountability partner either every morning or evening to give a report of what your goals are for the day and if you were able to meet those goals. If not, you give a brief explanation before moving on to listening to your partner. Both will take turns supporting one another and offering words of encouragement.

When choosing an accountability partner, think of someone that isn't your best friend. You need someone who is going to be strict about keeping you accountable and won't let things slide. Instead, you want someone to treat you like a teacher treats a student when they don't get their homework done. You want to be completely honest with this partner and not try to push anything under the rug.

Every morning when you talk with your accountability partner, let them know your list of five things you're going to get done. Then when it's time to check-in, explain which ones you were able to accomplish or when you plan to accomplish the tasks you didn't get to. Then you'll create that space for your partner as well. This creates a wave of motivation every time you talk to your partner, knowing that in 24 hours you'll have to give a report again.

REACH OUT FOR EXCEPTIONAL RESULTS

"Your support network is the solid ground from which you can propel yourself upwards."

—**Anna Barnes,** Australian author

Let others in your network know what you are trying to accomplish. The more you share your vision, the more chances you have of attracting the right people who will propel you to achieve exceptional results. Not so they can validate your ideas, but instead, share resources with you, present opportunities, lessons learned, mistakes to avoid, and connect you to the right people. They will also encourage you and share how proud they are of your choices. Words of encouragement really do go a long way.

I flew down to San Diego to help with a Jack Canfield training when I ran into a woman I had met before. She's the type of person who is so confident and comfortable in front of a camera. The way she dresses, how she can pose perfectly, and the constant excitement that she gives off.

She shared with me how she wasn't getting any results or new clients from Instagram. She ended up deactivating her account. I asked her what her goal was, and she said to inspire women. I shared with her how she was a huge inspiration to me. The reason I started working out regularly was because of her videos. The reason I hadn't missed a day of exercise was that she was being her true self and I could feel that. She was so thrilled and encouraged. At that moment I realized that she didn't have anyone encouraging her.

We all need words of encouragement. Be willing to reach out to express your goals and be willing to ask your friends what their goals are as well. Encourage one another, push each other to strive for big dreams, and always be comfortable reaching out for that support.

Activity 16.1: Time To Reevaluate

Look back through this book to review your life purpose statement, vision, goals, and affirmations. Decide now if they have changed. If so, take the time to revise them below. If they are the same, still write them once more.

Life purpose statement:

____

____

Vision:

____

____

Goals and Affirmations:

____

____

Area	Goal	Affirmation
1. Personal		
2. Professional		
3. Health		
4. Spiritual		
5. Finances		
6. Giving Back		
7. Hobbies		

Activity 16.2: Understanding Roadblocks

Review the Wheel of Wellbeing and look to see if there is anything that is stopping you from moving forward. List those roadblocks so you can start addressing them today.

Example: You've spent too much time hyper-focusing on your career that you haven't been creating time to spend on hobbies.

1. Personal life ______________________
2. Professional life ______________________
3. Health ______________________
4. Spiritual ______________________
5. Financial ______________________
6. Giving back ______________________
7. Hobbies ______________________

"Press on—nothing can take the place of persistence. Talent will not; nothing is more common than unsuccessful men with talent. Genius will not; rewarded genius is almost a proverb. Education will not; the world is full of educated derelicts. Perseverance and determination alone are omnipotent."

—**Calvin Coolidge,** 30th President of the United States

PART FIVE

Dealing With Self-Doubt In Your Pursuit of Ongoing Success and Wellbeing

Strategy 17. Navigate the Self-Doubt Or Lose Yourself

"Turning pro is a mindset. If we are struggling with fear, self-sabotage, procrastination, self-doubt, etc., the problem is, we're thinking like amateurs. Amateurs don't show up. Amateurs crap out. Amateurs let adversity defeat them. The pro thinks differently. He shows up, he does the work, he keeps on truckin', no matter what."

—**Steven Pressfield,** American author of historical fiction, non-fiction and screenplays

To lose yourself means to lose everything, including your belief in yourself. We will all experience self-doubt as we take action. Especially in the beginning, when you've never done something like this before because it's never been done before. It's easy to judge yourself, to think, "Who am I to be doing this?"

You might have already judged yourself as you've progressed through this book, thinking that you don't have what it takes to be successful. Or you might be worried you won't be able to remain dedicated to your purpose and vision. These are ANTs in your brain—Automatic Negative Thoughts. They add no value to you living a fulfilling life.

Know that self-doubt is a part of the journey. Just like we have moments of happiness and sadness, we have moments of self-doubt. One of my favorite sayings that I like to teach others is 'surf the urge'. Which means embracing self-doubt, acknowledging it, and watching those thoughts pass by. Let it go and then move on with a smile on.

You have a purpose, and you are born unique. This world needs you to fulfill your purpose and carry humanity forward. I, too, suffer from self-doubt. We all do. But don't spend over five minutes in that space. It lowers your vibrational frequency and affects your self-esteem.

When I received the director position for the digital publishing company, I asked myself, "Who am I to cold call CEOs and VPs? Why would they want to talk to me?" I had to overcome those thoughts and instead focus on the reality that I was offering value. I might not have known how to speak or have the right deep tone, but I was there to support them. They had a vision, and I believed in it. When I shifted to a service-oriented mindset, "I'm here to add value, I want to help you, I want to support you, I want to take you to the next level," things changed. It came down to focus and self-belief.

If you want to move from self-defeating to life-enhancing behaviors, I recommend reading *Get Out of Your Own Way* by Dr. Mark Goulston. It explains why we sabotage ourselves, going back to childhood origins of various behaviors. More importantly, it offers proven steps of action to transform behaviors that will enhance your life.

Everything that you are trying to accomplish is based on what you are focusing on and your self-belief. Without that focus, we tend to get lost. We move with the wind instead of standing still and being grounded. It takes practice to commit to your goal and stand with it till it comes to fruition. But the more you do it and surf through all thoughts of doubt, the easier it becomes to build your confidence and realize the amazing power that you possess.

SELF-BELIEF

Can you imagine yourself standing at the top of Mount Everest? What about hosting a major charity event at Times Square in New York City? How about owning a business that goes international within the first five years?

Some people can close their eyes and picture themselves doing these things and more. While others struggle with the idea, thinking those achievements and dreams are for the lucky few.

So how come you don't see yourself achieving these major accomplishments and more? It has everything to do with how you believe in yourself. This includes what you believe you are capable of achieving, the way you achieve success, and how many times you'll achieve success in your life.

Often, we seek external validation to prove that we are on the right path towards success. But the validation that matters the most is the one that comes from the still, small voice inside. At the end of your life, it will just be you and your thoughts. Take the time to cultivate a strong mindset where you are your biggest cheerleader. Believe not only in yourself but in that you can achieve anything that you set your mind to.

'If not me, then who?'

Yes, it's going to take time. It's going to be hard. But the reward is greater than anything you have yet to experience. So why not go for it? Remember, "If not me, then who?" You were destined for greatness and to serve others. It's exciting to think about how you'll serve, what you'll serve, and who you'll serve.

Do you ever wonder why you are confident in some areas of your life and yet in other areas, you have so much fear and self-doubt? The good news is that scientists have discovered the formula for how you can wire your brain for a more action-oriented kind of confidence that boosts your courage to act, even when you're feeling afraid. Positive psychology expert Louisa Jewell shows that adopting a resilient mindset will enable you to show up as your best self at home and in the workplace. Jewell has deep knowledge of the science of the good life, honed through years of study and practice, and in her book *Wire Your Brain for Confidence,* she presents only the most effective and proven techniques for increasing your grit and confidence.

Growing up, I used to play every sport possible, whether or not I was good at it. I would take part since I was the fastest runner in my school among all the girls. I won most track and field sports. One year towards the end of high school, a new girl joined the school. She was slightly faster at running than me. That year, after securing second place in 100 meters and 400 meters short distance running, I decided not to take part in the hurdle race. I had won those competitions for a decade. This was my first time not participating in the hurdle competition. As I watched her go, I realized she wasn't very good at the sport and I thought to myself, "Why would you not believe in yourself and just give it a try?!" She didn't end up winning that hurdle race. What a lesson learned!

Right now, you have the skills needed for success. Coupled with mindful living practices detailed in this book, you now know the secret to success. Never doubt the power that you possess. You are the foundation for every mega-success in history. You are worthy of this success as well. Read that again. You are worthy.

VALUE-DRIVEN

"Whatever your mind can conceive and believe, it can achieve."

—**Napoleon Hill,** American self-help author

Have you ever had thoughts like: "I'll never be good enough." "I'll never create as they do." "I'll never be able to speak in front of an audience." Do you get nervous about making a new connection or speaking up at a training seminar to share your own experience? These are normal thoughts and can be eased when you remind yourself that you are adding value to the lives of others. This is why it's important to draft your life purpose statement. To know that all your actions are in alignment with your purpose of serving people. Reviewing your purpose statement daily and visualizing how you are creating impact makes you jump through self-deprecating thoughts.

Think back to a time when you served someone else. This could have been at a food drive where you helped other volunteers receive food donations during the holiday season. Think of any time when you physically were serving others. How did you feel afterward? It might have been hard work during those few hours, but afterward, you felt amazing. It feels good to serve others and to know that you are giving back to your community.

This same feeling is what you can rely on when you are value-driven. It is no longer if you can achieve your goals, or if you can stay committed. The question you should be asking yourself now is how can I add value to the lives of those around me? When you are value-driven you shift from self-doubt to self-belief. The byproduct of service is success. It is a matter of time and consistent small action daily. Think not of *if* you can, but how you *will* add value in all of your action steps.

You can either navigate your self-doubt thoughts in real time or lose yourself completely and go off track. The choice is yours.

Activity 17: Self-Belief Affirmations

In this activity, think about all of the self-doubt thoughts you've been thinking about or have thought about since you started to write out your goals and create your action plan. List them all out below. Then, in the next part, rewrite all of your self-doubt thoughts into self-belief affirmations.

For example:

Self-doubt thought: I'm not experienced enough to publicly speak on a stage.

Affirmation: I am so happy and grateful to be sharing my story to inspire people.

Self-doubt thought: ______________________________

Affirmation: ______________________________

Self-doubt thought: ______________________________

Affirmation: ______________________________

Self-doubt thought: ______________________________

Affirmation: ______________________________

Self-doubt thought: ______________________________

Affirmation: ______________________________

Self-doubt thought: ______________________________

Affirmation: ______________________________

"We are what we repeatedly do. Excellence then, is not an act, but a habit."

—**Aristotle,** Greek philosopher and polymath

Strategy 18. Asking For Advice and Feedback

"Average players want to be left alone. Good players want to be coached. Great players want to be told the truth."

—**Doc Rivers**, American basketball coach

The idea that we can achieve success all on our own is a far stretch from reality. We all need help from time to time to be inspired, discover new ideas, and seek the motivation to move forward once more. We are not meant to do it alone. It is often the advice from experts and mentors that will uncover the solution to some of the biggest obstacles in your way. That's because they've been there, have overcome that same challenge, and can offer the solution.

SUCCESS IS A TEAM SPORT

Have you heard of or been that person who started a business and tried to do it all alone? Or have you been that person who refused to ask for help? Do you keep your ears closed when people around you give you feedback? Do you wonder why you are not progressing or getting the results you desire? Or perhaps have you ever had an intuition, ignored that internal voice and regretted it later?

I know I certainly have and learnt the importance of asking

for feedback—both externally and internally. External feedback is a gift we receive sometimes as a surprise or when we ask for it from others—your family, your partner, your children, your clients, your boss, the concierge, electrician, plumber, etc. On the other hand, internal feedback is the new knowledge one self-generates. Often, we call it 'a gut feeling' or 'intuition' or 'hunch'. Both these types of feedback allow you to gauge if you are on the right path or not and allow you to change your response to help get you to your desired goal.

As you set your eyes on your vision, you can see the destination you want to reach. You've created a plan and are now taking action to reach that place off in the distance. You will have people along the way that you want a part of this journey to help you or encourage you to get there. Or you may attract people on your journey who want to see you succeed, or they might distract you and get you off track. When we don't listen to the feedback, we stay stuck, and it delays us from experiencing fulfillment in the pursuit of achievement.

TYPES OF CONSTRUCTIVE FEEDBACK

There are four major types of constructive feedback. They include:

1. **Negative feedback–**
   Often, this type of feedback is the one that people avoid because they don't like to hear it. It makes them feel attacked, undervalued, and unmotivated. But they are simply corrective statements that inform us of what actions did not work, what should not be repeated, and what can be changed.

2. **Positive feedback–**
   This type of feedback reinforces past actions taken and allows you to be aware of what has worked. It creates higher levels of motivation and builds loyalty.

3. **Negative feed-forward–**
   They are comments provided to us about what actions should not be repeated in the future. These actions were unsuccessful and will not lead you to achieve your goal. It helps you take corrective actions in the present to align with the future success of your goal.
4. **Positive feed-forward–**
   They are affirming comments about what actions to continue in the future. These actions were successful and if continued, can improve your performance in pursuing achievement.

Really listen to what is being said. Evaluate if it applies to you. If it's a positive, negative, negative feed-forward or positive feed-forward, it is going to help you get back on course to reaching your goal. Even when you've ended up going in the other direction or have been completely turned around, continuously gaining feedback will help you stay your course.

ASK FOR ADVICE

"It's only after you've stepped outside your comfort zone that you begin to change, grow, and transform."

—**Roy T. Bennett,** author of *The Light in the Heart*

Conventional wisdom says you should ask your colleagues, friends, or family for feedback. However, research suggests that feedback can often have no (or even a negative) impact on our performance. This is because sometimes the feedback we receive is often *too vague*—it is not constructive and fails to highlight what we can improve on or how to improve. New Harvard research suggests a better approach. Across four experiments—including a field experiment conducted in an executive education classroom—researchers found people received more effective input when they asked for advice rather than feedback.

You'll find that while you are reaching for success, you're going to have to start many of the first steps. To find a mentor or build your network, you're going to have to be the first one to initiate conversation and offer something in return for their advice and support. When you want advice on the steps you are taking, you'll have to reach out for that input.

It doesn't always come naturally. You might feel shy to talk to friends or family about your goals, hoping to receive the type of advice or feedback you need to know if you're on the right track. The more you get into the habit of sharing your dreams with others, the easier it will become.

Asking for help and advice will eventually become such a natural part of your process of success that you won't think twice about joining a mastermind group or working with someone as your accountability partner. You'll come to discover for yourself that success can't happen when you're pushing forward all on your own. You'll need a dream team to rely on to ask for help and gain valuable advice and feedback. That is how you'll always hit the mark when reaching for your goals.

WHY FEEDBACK IS IMPORTANT

"Feedback is the breakfast of champions."

—**Ken Blanchard**, American author, business consultant, and motivational speaker

Giving and receiving effective feedback is a vital part of communication, whether inside or outside the boardroom, classroom, or in a family. Bob Dignen of Cambridge University explains, "Different aspects of communication lay claim to being the most important: listening effectively or building trust, for example. Though these are important, the critical skill for me is feedback, both giving and getting. Effective feedback has benefits for the giver, the receiver, and the wider organization."

Here are five reasons feedback is perhaps the most important communication skill.

1. **Feedback is there all the time–**
   It only takes a few seconds to ask a friend for advice.
2. Feedback is just another word for effective listening–
   Feedback means providing both aspects of effective listening, from showing understanding to expressing appreciation.
3. **Feedback is an opportunity to motivate or be motivated–**
   All types of constructive feedback are ways to self-motivate. It also gives you the opportunity to take a moment to express appreciation, to inspire others to do even better.
4. **Feedback is essential to develop performance–**
   Feedback is a supportive act intended to deal with under-performance constructively and to develop performance to a high level.
5. **Feedback is a way to keep learning–**

Invest time in asking and learning about how others experience spending time with you to develop new ways to share your perspective and create stronger relationships.

"The way a team plays as a whole determines its success."

—**Babe Ruth,** American baseball player

Activity 18: Assistance For Your Goal

Pick one goal that you are currently working on. Think about which areas you need help with in order to move forward with your goal. Do you need to gain a new skill set? Are you needing feedback or advice? Are you having a hard time staying motivated or thinking of additional action steps?

Example: I feel stuck in a relationship and am not sure what to do / I need help with building my website.

As you think about your goal, write what you need help with.

____

____

____

____

Next, think about who you can turn to for feedback or advice. It can be a support group, a mentor or teacher, a friend, or a family member.

Example: Your accountability partner, your mastermind group, your friends, or partner or children.

Who are you going to reach out to?

____

____

____

____

When you meet with that person, ask them, "How do you see me limiting myself?" Take the time to write about the feedback you received to start processing it and thinking of how you can utilize that feedback in accomplishing your goal.

Example: I see you limiting yourself by not networking enough.

____

____

____

____

What corrective action step will you take next?

Example: Read Aanchal Vash's book, *Ongoing Success and Well-being,* every day for 20 days to learn how to maintain wellbeing in the pursuit of achievement.

____

____

____

____

"We all need people who will give us feedback.
That's how we improve."

—**Bill Gates,** American business magnate

Strategy 19. Reject The Downers. Not Your Dreams.

"Letting go doesn't mean that you don't care about someone anymore. It's just realizing that the only person you really have control over is yourself."

—**Deborah Reber,** Fiction writer

It's going to become very noticeable when you start to relentlessly pursue ongoing success and wellbeing. What you are learning in this book and implementing into your daily routine is going to get the attention of others. Those around you are going to see how happier you are, the joy you are experiencing, and how motivated you are to reach new heights. They'll be so curious to know what the change is in your life, giving you the opportunity to teach others and encourage them to also learn the strategies in this book.

Your supporters and cheerleaders are going to be rooting for you each step of the way and providing you with words of encouragement. But those who are envious of you, perhaps jealous, will try to put you down because of the way they are feeling. They perhaps know nothing about living a purpose-driven life, how to align the Wheel of Wellbeing into your vision or how to be 100% in control. People who often react in negative or hurtful ways are the ones who want what you have. It rarely has anything to do with you. They simply want what you are working hard to achieve.

I know, it's the craziest natural phenomenon. We are all human and act based on the knowledge and wisdom we currently have. Therefore, it's important to ignore the noise and to keep pushing forward regardless of any negative naysayers or downers. Prepare yourself in advance to receive negative comments. As we discussed at the beginning of this book in the Author's Note, life comes with challenges. Living is navigating, problem-solving, and feeling joy. If you are going to work towards fulfillment in the pursuit of achievement, embrace that all sorts of people exist. Some are here to teach you, some to help support you and some are here to make you navigate your narrative of success and well-being.

What I've learned over the years is that not everyone graduates with a 90%. That means there are plenty of people who have jobs or businesses but are simply not that smart. They may have barely passed with a 49.90%.

When I worked with an estate lawyer to wrap up my late twin brother's legal paperwork, the lawyer treated me terribly. I was in a one-of-a-kind situation with my Canadian work permit expiring and me having to leave the country. I had the apartment to renovate and put up on rent. Figure out a way to change the ownership of Tushar's car to mine in order to sell it before I had to leave the country. These are just some challenges, to name a few.

I was adamant about problem-solving one step at a time and taking care of my wellbeing no matter what. After all, I had done nothing wrong. At that moment, I was trying to stay afloat daily.

So, I chose to reject the downer, not my dream. I found a new estate lawyer who communicated with compassion, responded to my queries effectively, and helped me secure the certificate of estate trustee.

DEALING WITH UNHEALTHY RELATIONSHIPS

"Do not justify, apologize for, or rationalize the healthy boundary you are setting. Do not argue. Just set the boundary calmly, firmly, clearly, and respectfully."

—**Crystal Andrus,** Self-discovery author

When you realize an unhealthy relationship in any of the seven areas of wellbeing, whether it's because the relationship has shifted due to your new success or it's been an ongoing problem, the first step is to set boundaries. I don't believe in canceling people, as you can easily click a few buttons to cancel your Netflix subscription. By setting boundaries, you're able to establish better communication.

To that person who may try to be a downer, make the choice to express how you are feeling when they speak to you like that. If the situation only worsens, make the choice to simply not spend time with them anymore. Saying no to their invitations is how you set healthy boundaries to protect yourself and your future of happiness.

These people still help teach us things about ourselves. We come to understand what we like and what we don't like. They teach us to be strong, to stand up for what we believe in, and to put our happiness first.

We have to define our next action step when faced with a demotivating experience. It's never okay to tolerate an unhealthy relationship, hoping one day it will become better. You'll never be able to 'change' someone or influence them to live a better life. They will have to discover that for themselves, just like you are taking the initiative to read this book and dedicate one day to each strategy. All you can hope to be is an example for others, to inspire them, and to serve them. For unhealthy relationships, that means setting specific boundaries that can't come down to ensure your own success and wellbeing.

"Our lives begin to end the day we become silent about things that matter."

—**Martin Luther King Jr.**, American Baptist minister, activist, spokesperson, and leader of the Civil Rights movement

When you face an unhealthy relationship, stop putting so much energy into that person. Direct your energy towards your goals or other people who fill up your cup. I had to learn this lesson for myself when I started seeking help and seeing a therapist. It took me meeting with several different therapists till I met one that was going to uplift me instead of trying to convince me to change my life that went against my beliefs. I was being heard, but not understood. But not every 'professional' scored a 90% in school. So, I gave myself permission to find another therapist that worked best for me instead of settling for the one before.

We want to help people grow and make an impact on our communities, but those downers have their unresolved problems. We can still help and encourage others, even those who created an unhealthy relationship with us. Be the change for yourself, and let others decide for themselves if they'll make that same change. Be that example for them, but never allow them to drive your dream.

Needing help in choosing the right words when dealing with a downer? Check out Renee Evenson's audiobook *Powerful Phrases for Dealing with Difficult People* which contains over 325 ready-to-use words and phrases for working with challenging personalities.

SETTING BOUNDARIES

"Life is too short to waste your time on people who don't respect, appreciate, and value you."

—**Roy T. Bennett**, author of *The Light in the Heart*

Be comfortable with unfollowing a person on social media if their content is bringing you down. You're not cutting them out of your life. Instead, you are quitting the channel of overcommunication and limiting your interaction with them.

I had to create boundaries with some childhood friends who added no value to my new life purpose. They were not encouraging and always passed awkward comments whenever I held self-help trainings. It was just not their scene. Over the years, I noticed how I did not enjoy the energy when I was around them. I found my body rejecting wanting to party or spend a lot of time with them. Something had changed. I no longer was looking for anyone's approval in what I was working towards. I had so much clarity in my purpose, that I didn't want anyone's negative energy throwing me off my game.

I know that healthy relationships start with me, and I am able to limit interactions as part of my boundaries. In fact, I realized boundaries can help save a relationship. So today I simply choose to not interact with them as much. I wish them so much joy and success, but they are simply not a part of my journey anymore. When we meet today through common friends, we have a great time together but otherwise, I don't have the time to welcome anything that doesn't add to the Wheel of Wellbeing.

RECOVERY IS UP TO YOU

We are all human. When you are in a difficult and troubling environment for far too long surrounded by toxic people, it does take a toll on your wellbeing, your will to practice self-care, your motivation levels, your ability to express empathy and so much more. It is up to you to choose to heal from the past trauma.

Healing is a part of maintaining your wellbeing in order to experience success. Jackson MacKenzie's book *Whole Again: Healing Your Heart and Rediscovering Your True Self After Toxic Relationships and Emotional Abuse* is one book that can help you on your healing journey. Jackson MacKenzie has helped millions of people in their struggle to understand the experience of toxic relationships. His first book, *Psychopath Free*, explained how to identify and survive an immediate situation. In this highly anticipated new book, he guides readers on what to do next—how to fully heal from abuse in order to find love and acceptance for the self and others.

Remember you can have success without wellbeing. But is that a fulfilling life and legacy you want to leave behind for generations to come? What will be your book of life narrative? You have everything it takes to decide today and create a life you enjoy living.

Reject the Downers. Not Your Dream.

"It is necessary, and even vital to set standards for your life and the people you allow in it."

—**Mandy Hale,** New York Times best-selling author and speaker

Activity 19:
Identify A Downer

Take the time to review your relationships and identify whether they are a downer or an optimist. Choose what action you will take to limit your interaction with the downer.

1. Social Connections

Name: ______________________ Downer/ Optimist ______________________

Actions I will take: ____

2. Professional Connections

Name: ______________________ Downer/ Optimist ______________________

Actions I will take: ____

3. Health Connections

Name: ______________________ Downer/ Optimist ______________________

Actions I will take: ____

4. Spiritual Connections

Name: ______________________ Downer/ Optimist ______________________

Actions I will take: ____

5. Financial Connections

Name: ______________________ Downer/ Optimist ______________________

Actions I will take: ____

6. Impact Creating Connections

Name: ______________________ Downer/ Optimist ______________________

Actions I will take: ____

7. Extracurricular Activites Connections

Name: ______________________ Downer/ Optimist ______________________

Actions I will take: ____

Strategy 20.
Rest. Don't Quit.

"Learn to relax. Your body is precious, as it houses your mind and spirit. Inner peace begins with a relaxed body."

—**Norman Vincent Peale**, Speaker and best-selling author of *The Power of Positive Thinking*

As you finish this book and spend this day reflecting on your journey so far, you've experienced the feeling of being inspired, deeply motivated, and building that self-belief that you can achieve anything you set your mind to. I'm so excited to hear about all the new goals you'll be accomplishing soon.

And while you've experienced a surge of energy as you start this new beginning, you may face moments of burnout, mental exhaustion, emptiness, devoid of motivation, or a sense of detachment. Know that this is a part of the process and most people who set a big vision experience it. They may not feel comfortable openly talking about it.

Look at all the daily work you are persistently choosing to do. There may be days when you consider giving up because you haven't seen the results you wanted to see, or they just haven't shown up at all. But you still keep going because you have the self-belief that you can make a difference. And I believe you can. I believe you are here to live your purpose and carry humanity forward.

We have seen it time and time again, the most successful

people we look up to who passed away by suicide—celebrity chef Anthony Bourdain, actor Stanley Adams, professional wrestler Mike Alfonso, Swedish DJ Avicii, lead singer of Linkin Park Chester Bennington, American actress Marilyn Monroe, and so many more. They pushed their limit to sustain achievement, but they were not well and didn't feel fulfilled.

What sets high achievers up for ongoing success and wellbeing is acknowledging that these moments occur and pursuing professional help. (The Bonus Strategy at the end of this book explains a methodology on how to respond to someone who is experiencing a difficult and challenging event, including burnout). High achievers learn to rest, travel, take a break, but they never quit. No one is going to tell you to rest. No one is going to come to rescue you or save you. You have to be the one to decide what is best for you.

Take the time to rekindle what sets the spark in you. Find out what makes you happy and do more of that. This is all a part of mastering yourself for your ongoing success and wellbeing. You will need to rest as you are working hard, but never give up on your purpose.

ME TIME

"There is virtue in work and there is virtue in rest. Use both and overlook neither."

—**Alan Cohen**, Author of 27 popular inspirational books

You often feel tired when you've done too much. You've probably experienced this by trying to take on too many projects while trying to juggle all of your responsibilities. The tired feeling comes from doing too little of what sparks a light in you.

I'm often reminded of this when I see mothers with their children. They sometimes look exhausted, as all the joy has been sucked out of them. Yes, they love their children. Yes, they are amazing mothers. But they don't take time to do something just for themselves. A lot of new moms go through this because they feel guilty taking time just "for me".

Take time for your own wellbeing without having any sort of guilt. There is nothing wrong with resting and recharging your own personal batteries. Tune in to what has been going on with your body and mind while you've just been on the go, go, go. You will start to become aware of areas that need your attention. Set time aside routinely to tune in and reflect on the seven areas of wellbeing.

Brianna Gilmartin from Verywell explains that there are different types of self-care: physical, social, mental, spiritual, and emotional.

- **Physical–**
  You need to take care of your body if you want it to run efficiently. Keep in mind that there's a strong connection between your body and your mind. When you're caring for your body, you'll think and feel better too.
- **Social–**
  Socialization is key to self-care. But, often, it's hard to make time for friends and it's easy to neglect your relationships when life gets busy. Close connections are important to your wellbeing.
- **Mental–**
  The way you think and the things that you're filling your mind with greatly influence your mental health. Mental self-care includes doing things that keep your mind sharp, like puzzles, or learning about a subject that fascinates you. You might find reading books or watching movies that inspire you fuel your mind.
- **Spiritual–**
  Research shows that a lifestyle including religion or spirituality is generally a healthier lifestyle. Nurturing your spirit, however, doesn't have to involve religion. It

can involve anything that helps you develop a deeper sense of meaning, understanding, or connection with the universe.

- **Emotional–**
  It's important to have healthy coping skills to deal with uncomfortable emotions, like anger, anxiety, and sadness. Emotional self-care may include activities that help you acknowledge and express your feelings regularly and safely.

It starts with setting aside an hour for yourself each day. Though this might sound intimidating when you don't practice any self-care routine, you'll soon discover how vital this one hour a day is to feel fulfilled. During that one hour, do things that spark joy in your life. Whether it is doing your hair or makeup, cleaning your workspace, or reading your favorite book, do it just for yourself and no one else.

As you practice this one hour of recharging your body and mind, acknowledge others to take 'me time' as well. Let your friends and family know how beneficial just one hour a day can be. We live in a culture where overworking is glorified. Be that example to those you care deeply for to also take time for themselves. As we encourage one another and grow with one another, we create a future brighter than anyone could truly imagine.

THE SMALL WINS

"Small wins are exactly what they sound like, and are part of how keystone habits create widespread changes."

—**Charles Duhigg**, author of *The Power of Habit: Why We Do What We Do, and How to Change*

Psychotherapist Martina Witter says we should still celebrate our achievements this year. Even if you feel you have little to celebrate. "Success is a journey, not a destination," Martina tells Metro.co.uk. "Celebrating small wins is critical to monitoring and tracking incremental accomplishments and achievements as it allows you to notice and pay attention to the present moment. Your journey of achievement is sometimes more important than the end goal."

Martina says that the small wins will position us for greater successes in the future. "We should accept and acknowledge the small wins as steppingstones and platforms to success."

You could incorporate more exercise into your day, and after a week of consistency, you're already seeing the difference in the energy you have each day. That is a small win.

You've started to include a healthy portion of vegetables into your meals and you're saying no to dessert to help feed your body and mind. That is a small win.

When asked to go out after work to socialize with coworkers, but you realize you just need 'me time', set those boundaries of saying no. That is a small win.

Take the first hour of the day to meditate and refocus on your purpose statement. That is a small win.

Becoming more aware of your needs instead of putting everyone first. That is a small win.

You are crushing it every day. Take the time to reflect on your small wins. They are happening all the time, and though they might not be the success you have set your eyes on, these are still moments of success.

This new beginning is teaching you so much about yourself and strengthening your belief that you can achieve anything. Allow yourself to realize that reading this book is a small win. Completing each activity is a small win. Personal growth is a small win. You got this! They add up to the big wins.

JOY IN THE JOURNEY

Every day there are moments filled with joy. If you have implemented the strategies from this book in your day-to-day and are doing things like following the triangle of power, 3–2 to-be to-do list, asking for advice, listening to feedback, and rejecting the downers, you are intentionally creating moments of joy. You are now not just relentlessly focused on work but on wellbeing and fulfillment.

You no longer have any excuse as to why you can't live a joyful life. When in doubt, choose an activity that will bring you joy. Feeling joy is a form of rest that your mind, body, and soul require to keep processing more information and tackle more challenges.

There is no reason you can't dream of being a singer, writer, poet, movie star, or a business owner. You are the author of your book. Set an intention today to add joy to your journey daily. Decide today that joy will be your guide. Choose to focus on joy daily. You are going to blossom into your true potential. Enjoy every moment as you become who you were meant to be all along.

"Success is not final, and failure is not fatal: it is the courage to continue that counts."

—**Winston Churchill**, Former Prime Minister of the United Kingdom

Activity 20: Acknowledge The Small Wins

To help with removing self-doubt from your mind, every single day acknowledge all of your small wins. For example, practicing mindfulness, drinking celery juice daily, waking up on time, exercising daily for 20 minutes, calling your parents every week or showing compassion to yourself. List all of your most recent wins.

1. ____________	11. ____________
2. ____________	12. ____________
3. ____________	13. ____________
4. ____________	14. ____________
5. ____________	15. ____________
6. ____________	16. ____________
7. ____________	17. ____________
8. ____________	18. ____________
9. ____________	19. ____________
10. ____________	20. ____________

Everyone who got to where they are had to begin where they were.”

—**Richard Paul Evans,** Best-selling author of *The Christmas Box*

Bonus Strategy. Supporting Someone Through A Difficult Or Troubling Situation

We live in a social world where connection is an important facet of sustaining wellbeing. When one person suffers, we all suffer. Whether that's the best-performing employee, your best friend, your partner, your sibling, or your child. When one suffers or is experiencing a difficult or troubling situation, it affects everyone around them in some form or the other.

Most people want to help and offer support. Sometimes the person experiencing a difficult or troubling event may not be receptive to the support. Or at times, the way we offer that support makes matters worse for them and impacts you directly. This is why at my mental health not-for-profit, Reach Out Together Foundation, I have created a methodology with the help of Disha Chhadva (School Psychologist) on how to respond to someone experiencing a tough time.

L.E.U.R.E. is the framework for having a confident conversation with family, friends, colleagues, and strangers who may be experiencing challenging times. Following this methodology will help you in assessing and navigating the troubling situation towards wellbeing.

1. Listen non-judgmentally

You may think to yourself, "I don't judge anyone." But we habitually make judgments about people based on their preferences, behaviors, appearances, and how they speak, eat, or choose to live. While it is normal for listening non-judgmentally, you must refrain from expressing those judgments as it comes in the way of supporting someone who is experiencing a tough situation. It is not helpful and often makes the situation worse.

If someone ends up sharing, we often pass statements like, "I understand how you feel. I too have gone through something similar. I was feeling like that just last month. You know what I did. I did XYZ . . . I spoke to this person." Or we may connect it to someone else's experience. By doing so, you make it about you or about someone else.

Did you really listen to what they shared? Do you believe they felt heard when you spoke? Probably not. It often happens when you are trying to find a response. So, you choose to connect it to yourself or someone you know. As a result, that person continues to feel unheard, unseen, and alone in their struggle.

Instead, it's more effective to create a space of trust by listening with full awareness. Don't fill in the gaps as they are speaking. Let them speak and listen intently. Make eye contact. If you're not clear, ask questions. Adopt an attitude of acceptance by respecting the person's feelings, not interrupting them, ridiculing them for why they feel the way they do, or disagreeing with them. This first phase requires you to create a safe space where the person's values and experience feel validated.

If they're reaching out to you or are willing to open up, chances are they want to share and be heard.

DO NOT: Read between the lines, fill in the gaps, make it about yourself, or disagree.

DO: Validate their feelings, create a safe space, and listen intently.

2. Empathize

Once you have created a safe space successfully, the next phase is to express empathy, which entails getting into their shoes and experiencing it like them. Take time to imagine yourself in their situation. This will bring out feelings of genuineness, which will help the person feel better and cared for.

Statements to use to express empathy:

> "I am so sorry this happened to you. It hurts me to see you in pain."
>
> "I wish I could take this pain away from you" or "I wish this never happened to you."
>
> "I understand how frustrating it can be to wait this long to get an answer."
>
> "I'm sorry you've had to deal with this."
>
> "I am proud of you for still choosing to show up every day. I can't imagine how you are feeling or how you have been coping with this."
>
> "I am here. Can I just sit here? I won't say anything. I just want to be here."
>
> "I am thinking about you."

> "I just wanted to send you a message/ voice note and let you know that you've been in my thoughts."
>
> "I can totally see why you would be upset."
>
> "I can't believe how well you're holding up, considering how much stress you're under."

From personal experience, I can vouch that these statements make a profound difference. When my twin brother passed away to suicide, I started hosting trainings to help different communities. For the first year, I held one training every month, along with participating in any external speaking opportunities that came my way. I was fueled to educate, support, and save lives.

I would often get a message from Erin Leslie, an EQ Coach and one of my dear friends, that said, "I am thinking about you. No need to reply. I just want you to know that I'm thinking about you." Those words silently were healing and often made me feel like someone out there understands that this is difficult. But I am trying.

Today I have gotten to a point where I empathize with myself and talk out loud to myself – "I am so sorry for what happened to you, Aanchal. You are a kind person. You have always meant well and done the right thing. I am going to do everything in my capacity to take care of you." I believe when you are going through that damage control phase or that difficult and troubling situation, you must have people in your circle that will not abandon you or tell you what to do. Rather, acknowledge you and empower you to make your own decisions.

3. Understand the problem

Assess the situation by asking probing questions. It's very human of us to feel reluctant and to avoid asking follow-up questions. But that is how you show genuine interest in the person's situation. Once you have assessed the mildness or severity, you then can respond appropriately.

Always stay away from your own experiences. Do not connect other people's situations with your own while understanding the problem. Setting prior experiences as benchmarks will once again make the person shut down. This problem is unique. Everyone is unique in their being and in how they respond. Not benchmarking their problem will build more trust and help you understand the problem better, which is necessary for the next phase.

Example: A parent reaching out because their teenager has been isolated, not attending classes, and doesn't have many friends left anymore. Even if you have been through a similar situation, avoid mentioning it and connecting it to theirs. Listen non-judgmentally, empathize, and ask probing questions to further understand the problem.

If you don't know how to assess the situation, remember you can always ask for help from your friends, teachers, coaches, professionals, experts, parents, or coworkers. You are not alone. Reach out to someone you can trust and who will again empathize with your situation. If the advice does not apply, remember to say, "next" until you find the right help.

4. Refer

If you are in this phase, it means the person is ready to accept help. You have successfully made them feel safe, secure, and in the right place. This is where, based on your discussion, you refer to resources you may know could help. The goal is to get them help.

Most people already have the answers, but they lack the encouragement, support, and will to pursue them. At this stage, if you recommend a resource or two, chances are they will open up more and say what needs to happen next.

In my case, as I had dived deep into being of service to others by participating in speaking engagements and hosting training events across the world, my Canadian work permit had expired. Even though I owned a condo, I didn't feel comfortable living there. My twin brother has passed away in that space and I knew I couldn't continue living there.

The only solution was to return to Toronto on a visitor's visa while I was hosting events, working on the Estate Trustee Without a Will paperwork with the Superior Court of Justice, Ministry of Finance, and Ministry of Transportation. To top that, I could not secure a rental apartment to live in. No one would approve my rental applications because I didn't have bi-weekly pay stubs. I was working for myself. I had 100% fully committed to my new realized purpose which brought me so much joy. But with so much coming at me all at once, there were moments of overwhelm when I was alone.

My friend Eric Madan, a Strategy Consulting Manager at a big firm, witnessed what I was experiencing, and one sunny day sent me an email. He expressed how proud he was of my choices to help others. He wanted to see me succeed and suggested 5–6 links to different therapists in the area. He also offered to make the first call and come with me to the first session.

This is a person who had never been to therapy before. He took the initiative to conduct research and draft a well-thought-out, sensitive email. I didn't ask for help. He merely put himself in my shoes, attended every training of mine, and concluded that this external support could help me sustain my efforts while maintaining my wellbeing. It brought me to tears. That was the start of my relentless pursuit of wellbeing.

Today, taking care of myself has become my favorite hobby. It empowers me to keep crushing my goals. Adding value to people's lives brings me so much joy. But I have to be the change *first.* I have to take care of myself *first.* I have to be full and complete *first* before I can be there for anyone else.

That is the power of planting a seed. You can make a difference by simply understanding the problem and referring people to the right support.

5. Encourage

Your support doesn't end at referring to resources. At times, people may find it difficult to wake up and get ready. Sometimes acknowledging their little efforts and strength makes an impact. Other ideas include picking up the phone and helping schedule an appointment, walking their dog, feeding their cat, cleaning their house, delivering groceries, or maybe sending flowers and a handwritten note. These acts of giving are encouraging to the person to pursue the solution to their troubling situation.

Three years ago, a young lady attended one of my training sessions on Mindset Mastery. I always request people to fill out a form online and submit it prior to the training so I have a better understanding of what they are looking to work on. She had shared little in that form. Initially, during our first few weekly classes, she was silent.

One day, I took her out for a quick snack after our training. She clutched my arm and started saying 4–5 things in a minute and none of them were related. I eventually realized she wasn't feeling well. She was always dressed professionally, laughed at my jokes, took part in the breakout sessions, and was fully present during the training.

I went through the entire L.E.U.R.E. methodology with her. From listening non-judgmentally, I learned she was in a tough working environment where her abusive ex-boyfriend was stalking her every move. He would send her messages with her photos, drive to her apartment wanting to pick her up for work, and as a result, she was not performing as well at work. She needed a safe space where she felt comfortable to be herself and let her armor down. She was longing for someone to acknowledge her situation and what she was experiencing.

After empathizing with her situation and understanding the problem more, she soon shared more details about her mental health condition. She explained how she was diagnosed with bipolar disorder and had been off her medication recently.

As I started to refer to some resources that I was aware of, she felt even more comfortable sharing that there was a hospital close by and they would give her the medication if she went into the emergency room. I decided to tag along with her to encourage her to pursue the help. We both went together to the ER at St. Michael's Hospital in Toronto, and she willingly accepted all the help the nurses were offering. She took her medications, got in a good nap, and eventually showered. She was smiling, and we had a great conversation for a few hours.

She continued to come to the weekly trainings, and at the end of the 3-month course; she shared some wins with everyone. One that made my day was that she gained the confidence to approach her manager. She shared what had been happening at work with her ex-boyfriend who worked on the same floor as her and how his behavior had not been making her feel safe at work. Her manager was always fond of her because she was always a high-performing individual. Her ex was transferred to a different subdivision and a different floor.

When you're trying to be there for your friend, sibling, or child, it's important to maintain a positive attitude and open mind in order to be truly supportive. The National Council for Mental Wellbeing shares the Mental Health First Aid tips to be an effective listener to those who are in need.

1. Reflect on your own state of mind: Before you can help someone with their concerns, be in the right frame of mind to listen without being judgmental. Ensure you're calm and ready to help.

2. Adopt an attitude of acceptance, genuineness, and empathy: Adopting an attitude of acceptance means respecting the person's feelings, personal values, and that their experience is valid. Even if you disagree with their values, put yourself in their place so you can be more genuine.

3. Use verbal skills to show that you're listening: You can use minimal prompts like "I see" and "ah" as a way to show that you are actively listening. This allows you to respond without interrupting them as they express their thoughts and feelings.

4. Maintain positive body language: Maintaining comfortable eye contact and sitting down instead of standing allows the person to know that you truly care.

5. Recognize cultural differences: If you are helping someone who has a different cultural background than you, you might need to adjust some verbal and non-verbal behaviors such as the level of eye contact or amount of personal space. Be prepared to seek advice from someone who shares a similar cultural background before engaging with this person.

These tips are just a starting point. You can consider becoming trained in Mental Health First Aid and learn other ways to listen and support those around you.

TERMS TO USE / AVOID

Below are some common phrases we hear about those who are not feeling well. In order to see change, we must first be the change. Let's change the narrative and learn to create safe spaces for open communication.

Don't Use	Use
1. Afflicted by mental illness, suffers from mental illness, or is a victim of mental illness.	1. Living with a mental illness.
2. A mentally ill person or a person who is mentally ill.	2. A person with a mental illness or a person living with a mental health condition.
3. Schizophrenic, psychotic, disturbed, or crazy.	3. A person living with schizophrenia, a person experiencing psychosis, disorientation, or hallucination.
4. Normal behavior.	4. Usual behavior or typical behavior.
5. Substance abuse.	5. Substance use disorder.
6. Committed suicide.	6. Died by suicide or lost by suicide.
7. Stop acting crazy or don't be insane.	7. Instead, focus on behaviors and their impact. **Example:** *When you don't clean up, the house gets smelly and messy.*
8. Calm down or don't sweat the small stuff.	8. This must be so hard for you, or I'm here if you want to talk about how you feel.

9. Therapy is for people who are weak. I just don't see the point of therapy or can't people just solve things on their own?	9. I'm not sure how I would handle what you're going through but if therapy seems a viable option that can help you, I'm all for it.
10. Things will be better in the morning or tomorrow is another day or cheer up.	10. That must really be rough to feel you messed up so badly. I'm here to listen.

This bonus strategy will help you approach and have confident conversations with a person in distress. It will teach you to respond in a safe and effective way to get them the help they need. Even if it is in the workplace—these strategies increase employee engagement, morale, job satisfaction, retention, productivity and reduce absenteeism, grievances, health costs, medical leave, and avoid workplace injuries.

To Your Ongoing Success and Wellbeing,
Aanchal Vash

Acknowledgments

I am enormously grateful to my mentor, Jack Canfield, co-creator of the billion-dollar *Chicken Soup for the Soul* book series. I first was acquainted with him through my late older brother, Prashant, who was an avid reader of all the *Chicken Soup for the Soul* books as they were published. Our home library was absolutely full of them. In fact, at the age of six, we three siblings started our very first business together. We opened up a library and charged our friends a small fee for using the library. Shortly after, my older brother started his next business of making labels, notebooks, and cards. My twin brother and I were his minions, and our salary used to be 2 items from each product we handmade. I have had the best memories growing up and I am certain it would not have been that way hadn't it been for all the hard work Jack Canfield and his team continued to do.

After my twin brother passed away, I was searching for a program that would certify me as a Success Trainer and give me the resources, community, and support to teach others concepts that have shaped my life. Lo-and-behold, I was getting targeted ads for his Train The Trainer program. I sent in an application right away. I was one of the youngest ones to apply, so I was told. It was one of the sweetest moments when I got to meet him and talk to him. It brought a lot of closure in real-time.

Meeting Jack Canfield made it clear to me how my older brother was so generous, loving, caring, and smart. I am in absolute awe of how he still continues to tirelessly come from a place of love and service. I have been fortunate to be on one of his assisting teams in San Diego and watched him make a massive impact on the lives of his participants. I am eternally grateful for his support, generosity, and mentorship.

Additionally, I owe an enormous amount of thanks to James Vanderlinden, the cofounder of Aware Ads, Oasis Ads, Fightful.com, and probably many more that I am unaware of. I first met James when he interviewed me for a job back in 2014 as an Account Manager. During the interview, I asked James about his success story and his vision. He was too humble and down to earth to acknowledge it as 'success'. He said that he didn't want a huge team and was happy with where the business was.

While I had the opportunity of working with him, his businesses kept expanding to a point where they got a whole new floor to accommodate the new team members. He lovingly named me 'Chilly', and I'd like to believe it was because of my work ethic and going above and beyond the role I was hired for.

James was instrumental in supporting and guiding me when my twin brother passed away. He helped me with an Estate Lawyer to work on the Certificate of Estate Trustee Without a Will, an immigration lawyer to help me renew my Canadian work permit, and a Real Estate lawyer to help transfer the property from both our names to just mine. He reached out to our local Member of Parliament on my behalf and got me an appointment to discuss my case. His generosity and strong leadership skills continue to be a source of inspiration for me. In fact, I remember James telling me about a book he had published on Amazon while I was working at Aware Ads. I was so moved by his dedication in exploring his potential. I remember saying to myself, "Boy! Is there something he hasn't done?" I am beyond grateful for a mentor like James and consider myself lucky to have him be a continued force of inspiration and guidance in my life.

A few other thanks: I am indebted to Ankita Paryani and Brad Northcote from my team. Ankita wears many hats—from Aanchal Vash Training to Reach Out Together Foundation, to now managing the Book Launch Team members. I appreciate her efforts, discipline, tenacity, and zest for making a difference in people's lives. Without her, I would not have been able to take dedicated time off to focus on writing this book. Besides her dedication to making a difference, the effort she puts in to be a good friend to those around her makes you want to be a better person.

I met Brad at my first 'Ongoing Success and Wellbeing' training event held in Toronto on World Reach Out Together Day on July 12, 2017. Brad was working at 680 News and had come to cover our event. He has never missed a single training held by me ever since. Brad has worked as a freelance journalist in Mississauga, Ontario, and continues to volunteer at any opportunity he can.

He believes communities work best when they're informed. He often says, '"When we each have the tools to reach our goals, we all benefit." In this light, he wants to bring academic knowledge and community voices together in pursuit of mental health and social health. Brad's humility, patience, and loyalty are tremendously valued. There have been days when work gets busier than normal. On those challenging days, Brad has been a rock for me. I am thankful that I have the chance to know, work with, and learn from him.

Similarly, I am thankful to the team who made this book possible – from the publisher, Kate Butler, and her guidance in this whole journey, the editor Erica Reed, my friend & psychologist Alinka Avendano whose support towards this book has been instrumental, to the members of the book launch team who read the book prior and contributed their feedback and excitement.

And of course, my parents, whose constant love, support, generosity, and never-ending kindness fuel me to dream bigger and push through all obstacles and roadblocks. After losing both their sons, the attitude they choose to keep, the love they choose to carry in their hearts for complete strangers, and their giving nature, continue to leave me speechless. I draw strength from watching how they both choose to move forward in togetherness. I am eternally grateful for role models like them to show me the path to ongoing success and wellbeing.

About the Author

Aanchal Vash is a two-time Amazon best-selling author, professional speaker, trainer, and entrepreneur. In 2022, she was recognized as the 'Top 10 Indian Women Leaders in Canada' by Women Entrepreneur India. In the last five years, she has organized and spoken at over 80 events in 28 countries across the world. She is the founder and Chief Executive Officer of Aanchal Vash Training, which trains entrepreneurs, impact drivers, thought leaders, students, and corporations in how to sustain fulfillment in the pursuit of achievement.

Aanchal was born in India, raised in Nigeria, and shaped in Canada. Her career started in Public Affairs at CitiBank, where she was selected for the Citi University Vacation Program in 2011. This program inspired Aanchal to help start-up entrepreneurs and thought leaders build strong digital brands; a business identity they feel proud of! Ever since, she continues to help leaders and industry experts build strong and profitable digital brands through Vash Media.

In 2016, after the loss of her twin brother to suicide, Aanchal changed her successful career as an Ad Operations Manager at an Ad Tech Network and become mental health first aid certified with the Mental Health Commission of Canada, where she had realized, there was a lack of basic mental health education in her community. She founded Reach Out Together Foundation, which provides mental health resources and training to students, young professionals, parents, community groups, and corporate leaders.

Aanchal started World Reach Out Together Day which is celebrated every year on July 12 to raise mental health awareness and spark a flame of hope. She has helped people feel connected, aware, rip their suicide notes, and reach out for professional help and other self-help supports through her annual conferences.

She has appeared on several media channels including – ABC, NBC, CBS, FOX, CBC's Metro Morning News, and the Hollywood Live TV Show. She has also appeared in a music video, 'I Won't Put Up With It' by Taylor Abrahamse, a Canadian singer. Her passion to create impact radiates through her personality and relentless advocacy of social work.

Aanchal received an EXPY® Award at the Annual Thought Leader Summit for her accomplishments as an entrepreneur, expert, and professional in California in 2018. She received the Community Development Award from the African Alumni Association, University of Toronto in 2019. In 2021 she received a Quilly® Award at the National Association of Best-selling Authors in California for her first book, *Success Strategies.*

You can connect with Aanchal via:

Email: info@aanchalvash.com
Social Media: @AanchalVash
Website: www.aanchalvash.com